The Light

A Book of Knowing

How to Shine Your Light Brighter
and Live in the Spiritual Heart

By Keidi Keating

...with chapters by 21 luminaries

The Light: A Book of Knowing
by Keidi Keating

Published 2017 by The Light Network
Copyright © Keidi Keating

Printed in the United States

Cover design by Tri Widyatmaka

Interior layout by Christi Koehl

Edited and compiled by Keidi Keating

ISBN: 978-0-9975727-1-1

Close your eyes and listen; certainly not to your head, preferably not even to your heart, but pay attention and listen very carefully to your Soul—the holder of all secrets, the library of all answers, the hub of all knowing...

Dedication

This book is dedicated to you, the reader, for your willingness and desire to be a brilliant beacon of Light, illuminating the way for others, and bringing hope and peace to humanity. May you continue to shine your Light brightly, as a beautiful lighthouse for the world!

Acknowledgments

Thank you to all the contributors of both this book and the first book in this series, *The Light: A Book of Wisdom*. Together we have created the most radiant Family of Light, which I feel infinitely blessed to be a part of.

May the Light rain down from the Heavens and touch everyone who reads this book to create a brighter, lighter, happier world.

Contents

Introduction

The Light comprises three books. The first is called *The Light: A Book of Wisdom*, the second is this one, *The Light: A Book of Knowing*, and the third and final book in the series is *The Light: A Book of Truth*. Each book ventures a little deeper into the Light of All That Is, and the entire set takes readers on an evolving journey to enlightenment for a true experience of our spiritual essence. These three books will be followed by a workbook, forming part of an online Light course and membership to an exclusive community of Lightworkers. For up-to-date information about this course and opportunity, please log on to *www.keidikeating.com* and enter your name and email address to receive future updates.

It's not necessary to read the three books in *The Light* series in order of *Wisdom, Knowing,* and *Truth,* however that's certainly recommended. If you're guided to read *A Book of Knowing,* and bypass *A Book of Wisdom* then trust your intuition, as perhaps your Soul is ready to access the deeper spiritual teachings. The process will be different for every reader, so simply feel in your heart what's right for you.

For those who haven't yet read *A Book of Wisdom,* here's a brief introduction about how I came to compile this series of *Light* books. It followed a comprehensive message from Spirit after I experienced a nine month spell of depression, desperate to know my life purpose on this planet. After asking God for a sign, an answer arrived in the space of 24-hours leading me to book a block of cellular healing sessions with a man called Richard Waterborn, who I met at a Mind Body Spirit event in Spain. Almost immediately after my first session I began to have profound spiritual experiences daily, such as hearing angels whisper my name, seeing Spirit and orbs of Light in the early hours of the morning, becoming increasingly psychic, leaving my body to travel to different realms, and even encountering alien-like energies. Needless to say life became very interesting! But after a while I realized that all this was essentially nothing more than phenomena: all well and good, and I did feel I was evolving spiritually, but instinctively I knew my journey had only begun. Clearly there was still much distance to travel on the road to enlightenment.

Whereas *The Light: A Book of Wisdom* set the scene for that journey and moved readers into the experience of some of that aforementioned phenomena, *The Light: A Book of Knowing* reaches even higher into Soul consciousness. It's from the inner depths of our heart that the Light shines at its brightest; the sacred sanctuary where we seem to intuitively know all of the answers, so that's what we're exploring throughout this book. Do you care to join me on a golden Soul journey full of Love, Light, and *Knowing*? Your adventure begins (or continues) here!

Love-infused blessings to each and every one of you,

Keidi Keating

become ever more beautiful. You will see."

The spiritual seeker smiled and looked down. There, by his side, were his rucksack and hiking shoes.

"Yes," said the Light being. "It's time for you to begin a new adventure. Come, follow me, as we explore Knowing and all of its luminous secrets…"

Section 1

Finding himself slumped against the familiar banyan tree, the traveler sensed his journey was about to begin.

He lifted a flask of water and took a large gulp while preparing both mentally and spiritually for the obstacles that inevitably lay ahead.

An elegant white butterfly flew across his line of vision and settled on a branch flapping its delicate wings. It stayed there for a moment, and a spark of light shone from its tiny antennae before it took off in the direction of the lighthouse, which was perched in the far distance upon a cliff.

In his heart the traveler now knew his adventure had officially begun.

Shining Your Light

☼

By Keidi Keating

Yeah we all shine on, like the moon, and the stars, and the sun.

~John Lennon

To me, living in the Light means making it a priority to bask in the magnificent sunshine of our Soul; that brilliant piece of God energy where pure loving resides. We are all made of Light at our core, and it's in this Light that the magic, joy, and beauty can be found. As little babies, our Light shines brightly because we are much closer to the Creator than when we grow into adults. As life progresses and we gain experiences in the world, encountering negative events and untrustworthy people, gradually we pull one dark cloak after another over our beingness, which dims our Light, until eventually it almost extinguishes completely. While we're trapped within the physical constraints of the human body, it's very difficult to experience the Light in its full glory. However, as we embark on our own healing journey, we may learn to let go of the cloaks one by one, until our inner Light is revealed to shine radiantly once more.

There are no words powerful enough in the dictionary to describe the Light, for it is beyond our comprehension as human beings. Take the most loved you've ever felt in your life and multiple it by about one million, and then you might begin to feel its potency and how transformative it is.

One of my favorite quotes is mentioned in the preface of this book: "When we take away all the material elements of the world—everything of matter—what we have left is everything that matters." In other words, rather than worshipping the materialistic parts of earthly existence, such as money and possessions, it'd be far wiser to spend more energy on the riches of life that our eyes may not see, but which are most definitely present. And the interesting thing is, when we make the switch from materialistic to invisible, the material side of things begins to take care of itself effortlessly, and we are ultimately given more than we ever dreamed possible. We simply have it backwards, having been conditioned throughout the centuries to think and act through fear, greed, and manipulation, none of which are so-called 'spiritual' attributes for the evolving Soul.

We are made of Light

When I awoke in the middle of the night to see an orb of brilliant white Light hovering at the side of my bed, it wasn't an ordinary light that my eyes are accustomed to seeing in everyday life. This was different. It was magnificent, made of Light beyond my logical comprehension. However, the Truth is that we are all made of this very same Light, and this Light is what threads all of life together in one unified tapestry. It's the same Light that those who have had Near Death Experiences (NDEs) and Out of Body Experiences (OBEs) often refer to. It's usually described as a never-ending ocean of pure Love. And that is God.

The reason we typically can't see the Universal Light with our eyes, is because we've been conditioned through the centuries (even in past lives that register deep down in the energetic of our body's cells) that such a concept is absurd and doesn't exist. And so we have a mental block that stops us from seeing that which we don't 'believe.' It was only after a series of cellular healing sessions, which literally shook out many of my own limiting beliefs and stagnant energy that no longer served me, that I began to see, hear, and feel Spirit and the Light on an alarmingly frequent basis. Alarming because suddenly a whole new part of life revealed itself and it felt somewhat disorientating for a while. I went from half heartedly believing to believing to knowing all in the space of two months!

Now is the time when we are all beginning to awaken to knowing, and part of this knowing is that you, I, and every other life force on this planet and neighboring planets is made of Light.

The significance of this information is that if the Light is God, and we are made of Light, then that must mean we are God, right? Basically, that is correct. We are all expressions of God. Every single one of us contains the energy of God. He expresses through us, as us, and when we pass on, we plunge back into that very same ocean of Love and Light and experience the blissful sense of oneness that NDE survivors, such as Anita Moorjani, speak of (see page 210 for Anita Moorjani's chapter *Stepping into the Light*). It's common for them to say, "I didn't want to come back to Earth," as they remember bathing in blissful Love having escaped the freedom of the prison we call the human body.

So if it's true beyond simply believing to knowing (and for me it is) that we are made of Light and we are all fragments of God energy, what does that mean for us and our lives in general? It means that, like God, we are all powerful creators. I'm not suggesting that destiny does not play a role in the unfolding of our individual journeys, but we are all responsible for the events of our life, and how we choose to perceive and react to those events. We are all able to manifest 'good' things by thinking 'good' thoughts. We literally attract what we put out there in the energy of our everyday thoughts. One trick is to witness what you are thinking, and realize that 'you' and the mind are two different things. You are not your mind. You are a Soul.

God speaks to us all a little differently,
hoping we'll tell each other.

God certainly spoke to me when the orb of Light appeared in my bedroom and told me to put together a *Book of Light* after I endured a spell of profound depression and 'asked' for a sign about my life purpose. And so I'm now passing that wisdom and knowing on to you, plus some ways in which I learned to reawaken my Divine inner spark, in the hopes that, like a game of telephone (Chinese whispers), it continues from one person to the next; from one spark of Light to another. Here are some of the ways I've learned to shine my Light more frequently and for longer periods of time:

Surrender and let go

By choosing to live in the Light, you will surrender completely to the Creator and refrain from planning your life to unfold in a particular way or seeking a specific outcome to whatever is in your awareness. By letting those feelings go the tension will no longer be present, allowing more positive experiences to flow into your life and your world. Tension literally creates a palpable barrier between your desires and dreams and God. When that barrier is present the blessings, which are destined to pour forth unto you, are unable to be delivered. It is only you who is stopping their arrival so the key is to get out of your own way.

Trust

Trust yourself and the Creator. He only wants what is best for you and so long as you remember that, trusting should be relatively easy. Remind yourself that He lives through you as you so obviously the only very best life experiences will come your way. And when self-perceived 'bad' experiences do occur in your life, look for the blessing as there's always at least one! From an early age we are conditioned by societal influences to be of a distrusting nature. We are taught to live in fear and never trust anyone. This is a very limiting way to live and remembering that what we focus on comes back to us, it's easy to acknowledge why many of us do attract these distrusting experiences in our life, thus reinforcing those programmed beliefs. A good place to start is by learning to trust yourself. Know wholeheartedly that you would never intentionally hurt another being in any way, and when you achieve that level of trust, you will then be able to trust others, too. And notice how from that point forward you will never encounter untrustworthy people or situations again.

Know

Knowing is the entire theme of this book as it's a step further along the spiritual path…and it's greater than wisdom, which was the theme of the first *Light* book in this series. We access knowing by tapping into the inner source that we all possess. It's difficult to describe where this knowing comes from, as it just is. Often it's wrapped up in the emotions, feelings, worries, anxieties, and materialistic elements of this world, which form a multi-layered cloak around our true being / our Light. As mentioned earlier, when we take off that cloak, layer by layer, true knowing will be felt. Knowing is greater than faith and trust…it's a step beyond those, heading into the realm of miracles and magic. Knowing is also associated with intuition and more can be read about that topic in the *Intuition and Knowing* chapter by Brandy Gillmore on page 34 of this book.

Love

To Love is a great way to shine your Light. Love every single day of your life without fail. Love the new people you meet. Love the motorist who pulls in front of you on the highway. Love those who challenge you. Love your friends, your relatives, your partner, and your animals. Love your enemies even, as that's an example of loving at its highest. Send Love to people you don't know in the street, to the checkout person in the supermarket, and even to trees, objects, and food; I like to sprinkle Light over my food before every meal! When you feel Love everyday and share it, the Light will reward you by sending Love back to you, which will be felt by every molecule of your being. I send Love to others by visualizing white or golden Light shooting out of my heart chakra, directly into theirs. Sometimes I even imagine the Love being wrapped up in a parcel and I witness the receiver opening it with glee! Let your creative imagination play when it comes to sending Love.

Meditate

Take time out each day to reflect, unwind, close your eyes, breathe slowly and deeply, and find the peace within. When you meditate you will attract people and experiences into your life which are resonate with you and your vision. The Universe also has a say in this, of course. So what you think your vision is, may not transpire to be what it truly is. I do my best to meditate three times a day: once in the morning, once in the afternoon, and in the evening before I go to bed. Like eating, it's better to meditate little and often rather than once a day for a longer period, as that way we break up our thought patterns more effectively leading to better results with our health, wellbeing, and the opportunities that flood our way.

Expand

Think expansive thoughts rather than restrictive ones. Always see yourself progressing and growing in life. See yourself as bigger and more successful than you already are. And remember, success looks different for everyone and doesn't necessarily mean more money, a bigger house, or a greater number of clients. It could simply mean peace of mind, freedom, and joy. Or, in my opinion, the grandest one of all: more loving in your life.

Relax

Rather than fret about your future, exhale and enjoy the present moment. Now is the only time we ever really have so fully immerse yourself in any task you do throughout each day, even if that's simply people watching or feeling the sun on your skin as you sit outside.

Ask

When I was stuck and depressed, the key to opening the doorway to my inner knowing transpired to be asking. One day I surrendered to my situation, looked up, and asked God for a sign. I was 100 percent present when I did this, totally engaged, and what occurred next was nothing short of miraculous. I received an answer—a sign—less than 24-hours later in the pages of a magazine, leading me to book cellular healing sessions, which transpired to be massively transformative and led to the creation of this series of *Light* books. So get into the habit of asking God for what you'd like, and always put your request into the Light for the highest good of all concerned. That way, you'll remain unattached to your request and, as an act of unselfishness, you'll see everyone involved benefiting for their own growth and betterment.

Give

One of the highest spiritual actions we can possibly partake in on this planet is giving. And I'm not just talking about giving money to a homeless person, or giving material items to your local children's hospice, though such acts are indeed kindhearted. I'm talking about giving of your Self. It's the invisible parts of life that hold the greatest power, and in giving of ourselves unconditionally through loving, compassion, time, and a listening ear, the Universe will always give back to us. Give away first that which you'd like to receive.

Following these steps will allow the Universe to work its magic in your life and lead you onto the path to achieve your wildest, deepest, truest dreams, which reflect the real you; your Soul.

Light Practice

Here are some actions you can practice daily, or whenever it feels right for you, to awaken your Divine Light further:

1.   Chant ancient Sanskrit hymns, such as the Kundalini Stavah, or recite short mantras, such as 'Om Namah Shivaya.' Your task is to research and find the chants or mantras that resonate with you. Recite them daily in

between your thoughts. For example, while you're sitting on the toilet, taking a shower, brushing your teeth, or sitting on a train.

2.   Do a form of Yoga daily. Find a form that feels right for you. My favorite is Kundalini Yoga as it awakens the serpent of energy that dwells at the base of our spine. That serpent, when awake, reaches up to the Divine and allows life to flow easily and positively.

3.   Develop a closer relationship with God through prayer and letting go of desires. Have enough faith to let God guide your life the way He sees fit for your Divine unfoldment.

4.   Eat healthy and nutritious foods, and drink fresh organic vegetable juices regularly. When we pay attention to what we're putting into our bodies, our energy field will strengthen and shine out into the Universe with greater potency. We will become like very strong magnets that can attract anything to us quickly.

5.   Be prepared to heal your past emotions when the opportunity presents itself. By healing yourself, you will help to heal the world at large. You could take a step now to research 'energy healers' or 'cellular healers' online and see if any resonate with you.

6.   Think positive thoughts and be aware of what you are thinking. Again, what we hold in our thoughts and our mind, determines our reality. There are many ways in which you can aid this, such as repeating affirmations daily, or creating a vision board—a poster made of images of all the things you want to be, do, and have in your life.

7.   Be grateful for everything that happens in your life,

even those things which you don't 'think' are favorable. See everything as a blessing.

I do not have all the answers about what form of Light awakening practices are right for you. Nevertheless, by simply setting the intention, the perfect methods and techniques will reveal themselves. You might find the answers in a book like this one, in the pages of a magazine, while searching the internet, as you're conversing with a friend, or in any other form.

Manifesting steps

During recent years there has been a great deal of speculation and interest in an ancient spiritual law modernly known as the Law of Attraction. Some people believe that simply by holding a desire or dream in their thoughts and focusing on it, that it will manifest in their reality. However, there is a lot more to manifestation than that, especially when we're manifesting from the higher laws of Spirit. It's important to remember that destiny also plays a part in our individual lifetimes on this planet and if something is not meant to come into our life for whatever reason, then it won't, at least not from the perspective of the higher Light. We may be able to manifest it from the lower levels of magnetic light, which can be controlled and manipulated, but that way it almost certainly will not be for our highest good or for the highest good of all concerned. For example, we might experience troubles or problems as a result of that manifestation or others may experience negativity. The best way I've found is that whenever we put a request out there to the Universe, finish with, "If it's for my highest good and the highest good of all concerned." That way if the ask does not fit that criteria, it won't manifest. However, be aware that you might receive something better than you'd thought about or imagined; something that does match the criteria in which you asked.

Manifestation story

What follows is a real life example of the Light at work.

Having lived in the same one-bed apartment on the Spanish coast for nine years, I wanted to move. However, I didn't want to pay rent in order to live somewhere else as I was still paying a mortgage and bills on my apartment. I asked the Light to help find me the ideal place to live, for the highest good of all concerned.

At this point I had no doubts whatsoever that I would be moving. I totally and wholeheartedly believed that it would happen, and soon.

I took this a step further and energetically showed the Universe I was ready to move by packing more or less all my possessions into boxes, and I really began to get into the feeling that I was moving house.

I carried on with life as usual and found that I didn't spare a second thought to all those items packed away into boxes. I did not feel attached to moving, nor did I wonder *how* it was going to happen. I simply allowed the Light to work its magic in whatever way it deemed to be for the highest good.

A couple of weeks later, a lady whose book I had edited wanted to meet about the possibility of getting it published. Her and her husband lived between Bahrain and Spain at the time. As I sat with them, sipping my peppermint tea, they told me how they desperately wanted to move to Bahrain on a more permanent basis, but they couldn't because they had to look after their elderly cat. They said they were asking around to see if they could find a reliable house-sitter but they hadn't come across the right person yet.

A Light sparked in my heart and I knew this was my opportunity. It felt so perfect and Divinely timed. I casually slipped into the conversation that I wanted to move house as I'd lived in the same place for the last nine years. They immediately asked if I'd be interested in house-sitting their villa in the Spanish countryside, which involved taking care of their 19-year-old cat.

A few days later I drove to their villa to take a look around. Two weeks later I officially moved in. It couldn't have been more perfect. The villa was gorgeous, the cat was adorable, and not only that, but they were paying me for the privilege! I had manifested exactly what I'd wanted (and more) and these were the steps:

1. I got absolutely clear on what I wanted to manifest.
2. I believed it would happen.
3. I put it in the Light and asked for it to happen for the highest good of all concerned.
4. I packed my possessions into boxes to energetically further develop the belief that this was definitely happening.
5. I stepped back and allowed the manifestation to occur.
6. I recognized the moment as soon as it turned up and took the appropriate action.
7. I said "thank you" all the way.

These are the only seven steps you need to take in order to manifest your deepest desires into your life, if they're right for you. Everything you want to happen is ready and waiting for you to energetically agree to it.

The reawakening of my own Light

Since my own Light reawakened after lying dormant for 30 years, my entire life has flourished exponentially. Magic sprinkled from the Heavens and I began to see the beauty— the Light—in everyone around me. Since the day that marked the beginning of my transformation, when I surrendered to God and asked for a sign, I've moved from Spain to the USA, married a spiritually evolved man, had a beautiful baby boy, started a new business, expanded an existing business, began living my Divine purpose, wrote several books, made countless new friends, felt happier than ever, and I've noticed an increased sense of inner peace and loving. I'm now far more aware of the Universal laws, paying attention to the messages in my dreams, looking out for signs and synchronicities in daily life, forgiving myself and others, and always putting loving first. Nowadays I live in a fascinating bubble of Love, Light, and miracles. My purpose right now is to simply share these revelations with others, so that's exactly what I'm doing through compiling this collection of *Light* books. My prayer to the Light in this timeless moment is that every single person reading this book, including you, begins to awaken to the Light of their Soul, shine brightly, and live a magical, fulfilling, loving life…for the highest good of all concerned.

Allow yourself to emerge from behind the clouds, and like a magnificent sun, shine your brilliant Light over the entire world.

~Keidi Keating

About Keidi Keating

Keidi is a spiritual author and mentor who supports people to connect to the Light of their Soul to manifest miracles and make dreams come true. She experienced a sudden spiritual awakening at the age of 30 after a series of transformational healing sessions. One night, an orb of glowing white Light appeared in her bedroom and instructed her to put together a Book of Light—called *The Light: A Book of Wisdom*—to assist and support others on their journeys to enlightenment. Following Divine guidance, she gathered 22 of the planet's greatest spiritual teachers and authors to contribute chapters, including luminaries and authors such as Don Miguel Ruiz and Neale Donald Walsch. The book is now available in seven languages, including Chinese, Russian, and Spanish.

The Light: A Book of Knowing (this book) came next, with chapters and teachings from luminaries including His Holiness the Dalai Lama, Anita Moorjani, Bruce Lipton, Dada Vaswani, and Pujya Swamiji. Keidi is currently writing and compiling the third book in the series, *The Light: A Book of Truth*.

Also a visionary entrepreneur, she is currently developing a couple of other projects to spread even more Light to the world.

For more information, *www.keidikeating.com*

And for book editing and publishing with Love and Light, *www.yourbookangel.com*

Igniting Your Inner Medicine

By Carlotta Mastrojanni

> *To the extent that the male initiate is able to nest into the magnetic fields with his Beloved and draw into himself the vibrational energies of these magnetics—to this extent he is making contact with Isis herself, the Cosmic Mother, the Creatrix of all time and space.*
> -**Mary Magdalene from**
> *The Magdalene Manuscript* **by Tom Kenyon**

I have always thought that our essence, that unfathomable instinctual part of us that is as unique as our thumbprints, lies somewhere deep within our sexual energy. It is here that our true power lies. Sometimes this energy is never fully awoken in us, keeping us separate from the deepest parts of ourselves that ultimately liberate us. Free from programming, guilt, and shame we are able to finally see who we really are. Far from the indoctrinated appropriateness of our behavior that numbs our instinct and reduces our choices, we can finally unleash our unhindered desire into the world and wake up to find that we are not really who we think we are. Orgasm* is the spark of creation. It is at the root of all transformation. When directed properly it allows us to become activated and strengthened as latent areas of consciousness and awareness are opened. The body is the vessel in which this alchemy can occur. All we need to do is bring our awareness to it. It is my belief that we were all born with the gift of clairsentience, with the ability to sense and feel into our environment and develop

*Orgasm is intended as the force of life that runs through everything. It is more akin to a continuously flowing 'orgasmic state' than to a brief sexual climax.

our sensitivity to it. Our body becomes our vehicle to tap into the world. The more connected we are to our bodies, the more we have cleared our channels to move emotions efficiently, the more pleasure we can derive from our life. As we expand our capacity to include the experience of life in its entirety, we access more power to manifest our desires.

Living my Truth

When I first started on this journey I had very little awareness of my body. I was always in my mind, processing, thinking, and rarely able to relax or to express myself authentically. I spent years feeling numb and the natural intuitive magic that I grew up with had long dissipated. I had a string of unhealthy relationships behind me and a terrifying hollowness inside that I couldn't explain. Worst of all I remained a mystery not only to others but to myself. I didn't know what I really wanted, much less why I didn't have the power to change the circumstances in my life that left me feeling alienated. Now I know that I was missing the signals my body was desperately trying to give me. Our bodies are, in fact, an extremely accurate instrument for gauging our Truth. When we are able to 'feel' the signs in a way that leaves no room for interpretation, it is much more likely that we will live in our Truth moment to moment, blessed with a more visceral, nourishing connection to ourselves and our environment.

By the grace of the Divine Light, the alchemist in me was ready to wake up. It was time to radically change my life. Finally, on a night like any other, as I was crossing the Trastevere Bridge in Rome, I saw a poster for a special kind of yoga that promised to awaken the senses and bring awareness. The very next day, I was in a Kundalini Yoga class, and before long I began to teach it. I cleared the pathways of my body enough for more Light to come through. My nervous system strengthened every day, and so did my willpower. I knew exactly how to angle my neck and curve my spine to follow the flow of energy. Heightened experiences with subtler energetic dimensions were the order of the day. I became stronger and bolder...yet still, something was missing. I felt alone behind an impenetrable glass wall. I was now connected to my Higher Self, yet still unable to express myself, and whilst I wasn't sure how to stop hiding, I was desperate to connect with others at a much deeper level.

That's when Orgasm found me. Orgasm not as in sexual climax, but as in the force of life that runs through everything. I was practicing a meditation involving orgasmic energy that cultivated its flow in my system, and in a short amount of time, it began to course through me and the floodgates opened. I had the full force of what is sometimes known as the Chi of the Taoists, the magical Sekhem of the Egyptians or the Shakti of the Eastern traditions suddenly run through me. A secret fire had been ignited within. I remember its force was such that it took me down with a fever, which lasted for two weeks! When I re-emerged into the world it was as though this secret fire had taken over my body. This inner energy was like an endless source of mostly untapped power that I quickly realized, if cultivated, could be the difference between the average version of me and the superhuman super-powered badass version of me. I called this newfound power my 'medicine' and I drank this medicine as frequently as I could. I kindled my fire day and night. My body was hungry for it and I wanted to be saturated by it fully...it was life force energy that was quickly unsticking all of the negativity I was holding onto. I went into deep corners of my ego, into shame and pride and resentment, so that I could transform and release all of the energy that was keeping the Orgasm from flowing freely, and keeping me separate from my Self. I was grateful for the years of practicing Kundalini Yoga. It proved essential that my body had been skillfully prepared for what was to come. I continued doing intentional meditations to move this sexual energy throughout my body. Since energy flows where attention goes, I worked with visualizations and techniques to direct my awareness to specific parts of my body to cultivate the heat that had ignited my whole system.

Fear and desire

For the first time in my life, instead of turning a blind eye to my shadow and trying to 'purify' myself, I discovered that all I needed to do was include the unwanted feelings into my system to alchemize them. I discovered that in the center of my belly there is a crucible that transforms the cold winds of fear into flames of exhilarating desire. Fear and desire, as it turns out, are the two sides of the same coin. My experimentation with Orgasm continued and I quickly found that more impurities were blasted right out of my system. A hidden part of me arose like the phoenix from the flames, brand new, and with the Light of Orgasm emanating from my eyes. My mental faculties were polished, and my capacity to contain more desire, more emotion and more of my unique essence greatly increased.

A different kind of knowing had begun to take place in my body. Desire became my Compass for Truth. It was a visceral knowing that I could not escape. Through yoga I had an exact technology for producing precise results in my body, but it wasn't until now that I could know the Truth in every muscle and sinew. My body could tell me with pinpoint precision the next right thing to do and say, and then the next right thing. And so I went on, living more from the depths of my animal instinct than my mind; living removed from the stifling should have's and could have's that kill Orgasm and more in my authentic self. As a result, my creativity began to explode. Suddenly every feeling in my body had a location, a texture, and a color. Deeper and deeper I ventured into the magic of my inner world until I realized the alchemy wasn't only happening within my body; it was happening all around me, in nature too. The hot flushing of my cheeks was the same as the crackling of a fire raging, autumn leaves softly falling to the ground, or a bubbling hot spring. All of life revealed itself to be in constant synergy and motion, in an orgasmic state of being.

Becoming an Alchemist

Within time, I developed my skills as an Alchemist and I discovered that Mother Earth and I had something in common. In all Alchemy there are three main components: there is a container, something that needs transforming, and a temperature that provokes the transformation. The greatest container of all is Mother Earth, and Orgasm, the sexual and creative energy, is the same heat that transforms our bodies and nature itself. Now that I have learned to thrive from my secret fire, I have become an acute self-sensory being. A shape-shifter of sorts. I know it when I feel the bite of painful news around my heart, the trace of electricity across my belly with my lover's touch, the fogginess that descends on my mind when my Truth is not in resonance with my words. I have learned over time when it is time to run, to accelerate, to slow down, and to pause. This kind of sensitivity is the birthright of every human being. We have simply buried it under so much numbing and so many years of not being asked what we really want, that we don't even know what our desire is anymore. The smallest things have now become the most radical tools for waking up, such as knowing I want the vanilla ice cream instead of the chocolate chip, and saying no instead of yes when I really mean it.

Orgasm and the Earth

Orgasm is the feminine creative principal that is the fuel for our lives, yet in order to be effective we must reconnect not only to our bodies but also to the wisdom of the Earth. All of life is in constant communication with us. There is an oracle behind every bird cry, every pattern of light on a rock. All we need do is open our senses and learn to read the signs. In

Native American cultures, when a child came out of the womb, its body would immediately touch the ground, connecting to the grounding and nourishing resonance of the Earth. That resonance would last a lifetime and be a guiding force like a perpetual drum call back home. I have been fortunate to be a part of a community here in Ojai, California called Earth Walk. Through the shamanic teachings I received from the elders, the Earth's energy began to open up to me, and I experienced the orgasmic state of nature in deeper ways, only this time, it began to talk back to me. I was flowing with the intelligence of the Universe. Orgasm and the Earth are both feminine principles. They both beckon us into their realm of oracular knowing, feeling, and mystery. One is the creative fire and spirit, and the other the grounding container. I began to work with both together. You see, Mother Nature holds us when we decide to go through the alchemical transformation from the old to the new. By keeping us centered, she makes sure that the power we have cultivated through orgasmic practice is grounded in purpose and put to good use.

Orgasm is my inner Light. It has taught me to channel sexual energy through my being to be a beacon of joy and radiance. I have become more connectable and more tuned in, more at ease with the flux of life. Orgasm allows my mind to be more fluid and my body to resonate like a tuning fork so that I may see things as they are and not as I wish them to be. I have become friends with the unknown, finding a sense of knowing within, and welcoming life as it is rather than wanting to be in control of it. My Orgasm is not dependent on anything or anyone else. It is not given to me, and no one can take it from me. It is an unending force that keeps me full if I have the desire to cultivate it. Everyone has their own particular flavor, what I like to call their own brand of medicine. Mine is wild, smooth, deep, and earthy. It rises from the Earth like magic ivy cloaking everything with sparkling golden Light and magnetizing even the whispers in the wind. It tastes like the turquoise ocean and smells like roses and cloves.

Light Practices

Take a moment to feel into your body. Have you ever asked yourself what your essence, your medicine, your unique spark of Light might be?

Here are a few Light Practices to help you connect with yours:

1. Cultivate attention: Begin to think of yourself as a pleasure body; a being able to feel with pinpoint precision what is happening within you at all times. Not only that you are hungry or sleepy but how did that conversation feel in your body? Did your cheeks burn? Did your gut tighten? Did you feel a prickly cold travel through your veins? The sensations you are feeling are your Orgasm. That is your body speaking to you through the nuances of your temperature and skin. Keep your attention on the sensations in your body and eventually the messages will begin to come through loud and clear, and your desire will let you know the next right step for you. Your body doesn't lie and your Truth feels like a tsunami of electricity enveloping your body. You will develop clear sight because you will be able to resonate with the Truth of everything around you and see things as they really are, not as you wish them to be. Visualizations in orgasmic practice are also extremely effective. Remember, energy flows where attention goes. Put your undivided, exquisite attention on your left hand now. Can you feel the sensation increase? Now put your attention on your pelvic area and breathe deep to collect energy there. As the energy builds, imagine a cobra moving from the root of your spine up to the top of your head until it opens its hood to cover your crown. What are the sensations at the top of your head now? This practice is one simple yet effective ancient alchemical technique to cultivate Orgasm.

2. Have a desire practice: be sure to make requests based on your inner knowing. And if you don't have a clue, fake it until you make it. Be precise about what you're asking for and be decisive. The next time someone offers you a cup of tea, receive it with your full self. Get used to asking for it exactly as you want it. If it's steeped for three minutes with a splash of milk and a drop of honey on the side, go ahead and ask for that! Revel in having your desires fulfilled. You deserve it. We have become unaccustomed to receiving and these small efforts to push out allow us to open the door to bigger desires and to the knowledge that we are being seen and heard. We must begin to trust what we are feeling and to trust that it is safe to express it in words. It's important to allow other people to feel safe too when they are communicating with us. This keeps the channels open and allows for greater intimacy. Relationships are the ultimate alchemical container for transformation. Learning to be in the heat of transformation without running from it is one of the greatest gifts you can ever give yourself. If I had only one rule it would be to stay connected no matter what. That way you can stick around to see the real magic happen, beyond the fear and pain, where freedom lies. A vastly important part of orgasmic practice is the cultivation of an open heart. The heart is the true gateway through which everything can be accessed and transformed. Love is what allows life to flourish and it is what we must plug into so that our newfound power doesn't succumb to force or manipulation, but instead grows into devotion and inspiration.

3. Turn your fears into desires: Getting to know yourself is the greatest source of power there is, so explore. Follow the thread of your desire. When your body is giving you signals, get curious about what lies beneath the sensation. Dive in as deep as you can. Don't be afraid to go into the shadowy parts of yourself as well, as that's where the juicy growth

is. Your fear and shame and other negative emotions are like pockets of energy holding the real you hostage. Once you discover what the desire beneath the fear is, you will create more space in your system for the real you to inhabit your body. Truly being in approval of your emotions and feeling them fully is what allows them to turn into gold. A good place to start is by journaling on a sensation that has come up for you. How does it feel in your body? How can you radically shift your perspective to be 'turned on' by the feeling instead of repulsed? How can you reframe it by looking inwards and taking responsibility for it instead of falling for the dynamic of blame and shame? Liberate your desire so the creative force of your Orgasm can be free to magnetize your highest good to you!

4. Ground in the Earth: Imagine the color of the Earth's energy is red. Every time you feel overwhelmed or stressed or need extra grounding, consciously 'run red' in your system, allowing her resonance into your body fully. Also, in going outside and planting your feet firmly on the ground, you can give back to her some of the energy that you want to release for her to alchemize in return. Then if you have your attention out enough, you will feel her energizing you with the vibration of her sounds and landscapes that become electricity and charge your whole being. You may find that messages register within your body or perhaps her unique harmonics stimulate brainwave frequencies associated with active imagination and dreamtime. Either way, stay intently present. Oracles stream in from the everyday world around us, and once you feel kinship with All That Is, it is impossible to feel alone or confused. The Earth's energy is so simple to connect to yet astounding in its power to transform our wellbeing. If you're not able to go outside and put your feet directly on the ground, you can buy grounding tools that connect you to the electrical frequency of the Earth establishing the healthy conductivity between your body and the Earth.

Conclusion

The Earth teaches you how to ground into your physical reality so you can be steady and clear enough to fulfill your purpose. Without purpose, the power cultivated through orgasmic practice can be left flailing like a disconnected cord. Orgasm allows us to become full again, and once we are living from a place of overflow, rather than lack or hunger, it is much easier to give back to the world. In fact, once your body is so saturated, you will find that you will need to put your attention out and find ways to give back. How amazing would the world be if we were all living from this place, free from our emotional turmoil and living life as if it were a succession of sensations that are neither good nor bad in themselves, but simply stories and experiences to be felt, cherished, and alchemized?

When you are saturated with the gift of your unique inner Light, feeling turned on and connected, you will be secure in who you are and ready to communicate your True Self to the world. Your Orgasm is your medicine. It is the root of your power and your emotional freedom. It is your unhindered artistic expression. It is your radiance and your magnet. It is your return home.

A Shaman uses sound, breath, and movement to tap into the world. The Earth, the great Cosmic Mother, speaks to us at every turn, if only we can tune in with our minds, bodies, hearts, and souls.
~Carlotta Mastrojanni

About Carlotta Mastrojanni

Carlotta is a modern day curandera and creator of Secret Fire, a shamanic coaching program born of over ten years' experience teaching the esoteric arts in Europe and the US.

She has developed her own unique awakening process called 'Love Alchemy' that combines both the power of Orgasm and Earth Energy. Her mission is to unlock the orgasmic secrets of Mother Earth that lie deep within your body and turn up your natural superpowers of intuition, sensing, and feeling so you can ignite your power and freedom.

When Carlotta is not teaching you can find her traveling across the world, living with tribes and making documentaries on subjects she is passionate about. Her films have been internationally acclaimed in different continents, and Carlotta thrives in bringing ancient indigenous knowledge back home so we may all ignite our own medicine and become our own shamans.

For more information, *www.whatsyourmedicine.com*

Intuition and Knowing

By Brandy Gillmore

*Have the courage to follow your heart and intuition. They
somehow already know what you truly want to become.
Everything else is secondary.*

~**Steve Jobs**

What would your life be like if you could find the answer
to turn around every situation in which you feel
physical or emotional pain? Right now, wherever you are in
your life this might sound impossible. However, in Truth,
there is an answer that will help you get out of whatever pain
you may be in, no matter how severe. I know because I've
been there. I've experienced physical pain that was medically
identified as the worst possible physical pain a person can feel.
The medical system gave up on me. But I found my way out
through learning how to follow my intuition.

Learning how to follow your own intuition is not only the
key to leaving physical or emotional pain behind, but also to
creating happiness, success, fulfillment, and expanding your
consciousness. Intuition is an impulse or communication of
information we receive from outside of ourselves; a guiding
Light available to every human being. Where does it come
from? Life, the Universe, God, Higher Power, or however you
describe Source energy.

Whether you are in hardship and reaching for the answers to
get through a painful experience, or you are at the leading edge of
conscious growth, my intention for you as you read this chapter
is to further explain what intuition is and share with you how to
develop and deepen your connection to your own intuition. As
you learn how to connect to your intuition in this much deeper

way, the benefits to you will be truly life-changing.

Some people discover their connection to intuition easily and naturally, but do not use it to its full ability. Others struggle to connect to it or are completely unaware of it. Unfortunately, many people experience severe hardship, which brings them to a place where they finally decide to tap into and receive the gift of their intuition. If you've been brought to your knees in a place of surrender, following your intuition can turn around your entire situation This was the case in my own life.

Developing my intuition

My journey to developing a stronger intuition started with a devastating illness. I found myself in a place I never thought I would be—lying in bed in extreme pain, propped up on pillows, surrounded by medical equipment. I felt desperate to find the answer—any answer—to get my life back.

I never imagined I would be someone who was sick, stuck in bed, or in a wheelchair. I'd always been independent. Yet here I was with a multiple diagnosis that included Complex Regional Pain Syndrome (CRPS), nerve lesions, spinal fractures, Spondylosis, and a few others. CRPS is known to be one of the most painful chronic conditions a human can experience. Despite being on heavy medications, it felt like razors and burning coals were stuck in every inch of my body.

For several years, I was confined to bed, in and out of hospitals, and I worked with every specialist I could find. I went to each appointment thinking this would be the doctor who would fix me. Yet every appointment ended the same way: choking back my tears and begging the doctor for a referral to someone who could help. Each doctor said there was nothing they could do. For five years I lay in bed, frantically researching, trying to figure it out. Finally, I hit my breaking point.

I lay there without even wanting to open my eyes. I thought to myself, *what is the point?* I had tried every medical procedure, diet, supplement, and everything I could find, yet still nothing worked. There didn't seem to be a way out. The thoughts that followed were so dark they scared me. In that moment I knew that if I wanted to live, I had to do something different.

I realized that if I listened to what everyone else was saying, there was no hope of ever getting better. So, I chose to stop listening to what everyone else was saying and stop trying to get better. Instead, I decided to focus on how to get through the present moment. I asked myself, "What do I need right now?" And I began to look within. As I asked myself this question, I found the voice that mattered most—my intuition.

The voice of my intuition wasn't a profound, booming voice; it was subtle, like a gentle guiding light that seemed to know its way. Lying in bed, I had no other options available to me and nothing left to lose, so I surrendered to this guidance. It led me through one moment, and then another and another. The more I listened, the more information came through.

Through this process, I became aware of a sense of knowing that the answers for my healing were inside of me. I began to explore my subconscious mind. Through trial and error, I discovered a way to interact with the subconscious mind that positively affected my health. I implemented this process each day, and the pain in my body began to subside. For the first time in more than five years, I felt like I could breathe again. I continued to get better and better at listening to my intuition and my body began to heal! I practiced walking every day. At first, only short distances. But then real strength returned to my body and my whole world changed.

Following the guiding light of my intuition not only gave me back my life and my health, but it changed my entire life for the better. Everything changed—from my health, my level of happiness and security in life, to my relationships, my finances, and the entire way that I looked at, and understood the world.

Today, I can't imagine living without my intuition. It has

become a regular sense to me, like smelling, seeing or hearing. Having strong intuition is so huge that I would not take back what I went through because of this gift that emerged.

After developing my intuition, I also developed an intense hypersensitivity to energy that enables me to feel what others are feeling. If you have ever heard before that a dog can sense fear, it's like that. Or similar to what the medical community would call mirror touch synesthesia, where one person can feel what another person is feeling. Using this in addition to my intuition has transformed my entire life.

What has become normal for me looks like a miracle to most people. For example, I regularly show people how to get out of chronic pain in minutes and make changes to their health and their lives using the power of their own minds— often in front of large audiences. After a person experiences how quickly their physical pain is dissolved, I always ask, "What else are you capable of that you didn't know you could do?" The truth is that you are far more amazing than you realize; your brain simply doesn't know it yet.

Where does intuition come from?

Intuition is a data-stream that comes to us from the Universe. We all have the ability to connect to it, even though we can't see it. We can't see wi-fi, gravity, wind, or even a song playing on the radio, yet we know they are there. When we stop and think about it, we know that intuition is present when we look at animals in nature. They use intuition, their innate "wi-fi" all the time. Of course there is animal instinct—each animal knows what to eat, when and how to breed, and they each have their set of regular behaviors. However, what I am referring to is real-time information, such as knowing when a flood, earthquake, or tornado is about to happen. Many researchers have studied animals and birds and watched that all leave a region abruptly, only to discover that a tornado hit the next day. This is an example of showing that this Universal "wi-fi" is everywhere, and how valuable intuition is in their lives and in our own lives when we learn how to tap into it and listen to it.

Using intuition in your life

Since intuition is active, real-time information coming from the Universe, it is constantly guiding us. Whatever the data-stream sends us, our intuition always leads us to our highest good. We can depend on that. Not only does intuition help us stay on a path of our highest good, it also empowers us to be our best selves.

The information we receive from our intuition can take us to magnificent paths we never dreamed of. If you're already on a good road, that's great, but intuition can take you onto an even better one. Or it can help guide you away from danger. Similar to the way animals leave an area when a tornado is approaching, intuition can also help to steer your life to avoid potentially devastating circumstances.

Intuition can direct the smallest things in your life, such as what to eat or where to stop for gas, to the work you do in the world—and every aspect of your life in between. Intuition can also help in your day-to-day interactions with other people. Your intuition will guide you to knowing who the right people are for you to do business with, to date, or to cultivate as friends.

Your intuition may also give you confirmation that you need to take action, or you might receive a message to stop and go no further. We've all heard someone say, "I had a bad feeling about getting into that relationship. Something felt off, but I did it anyway." When you start to develop a connection with your intuition, in a situation such as this, it becomes much easier to discern whether or not you are nervous because it's a new relationship, or if your guidance is telling you to run in the other direction.

If you learn to develop your intuition when it comes to the little things, you can experience how trustworthy your intuition really is, and then the more you will listen to it concerning matters of great importance.

How does intuition communicate with us?

Intuition can show up in a variety of ways—as a gut feeling, as a vision, something we "hear," or a strong sense of knowing. We need to realize that the way it shows up is not as important as the message it is trying to deliver. Think of it this way: if you were trying to tell a friend to watch out because someone in their life was not good for her, it would not matter if you told her via text, email, snail mail, called her, or in person, as long as you got the message across in a sincere and caring way. It is all data being broadcast in one way or another. The same is true with intuition. The message content is important—not how you send it or receive it.

Intuition is like the internet because there is a two-way connection—we can receive information from the data-stream, and we can also ask questions to get the answers we are searching for. People who already have preconceived answers don't keep looking for other answers. However, people who are at the end of their own knowledge are ready to surrender to an answer from their data-stream.

Connecting with your own intuition

Remember when you first started navigating the internet? You were probably unfamiliar with it, and it may have taken a little time to learn. But the more you used it, the easier it became. The same is true for learning how to connect to your intuition.

The first step is to realize that you do have this capability, as does everyone. The next step is to discover how your brain and your body process the information from your intuition. Developing your intuition is often consistent with your brain's primary way of learning and processing information, be it visual, auditory, or kinesthetic (feeling).

Often, when people get a vision, they expect it to be like a TV broadcast. However, a vision doesn't need to be seen clearly, like a high definition movie. Many times, visions have more of a holographic look. Similarly, audio messages aren't necessarily a voice that can be heard, but more a "feeling" of a voice, similar to a thought. For people who are more kinesthetic (feeling-oriented), it takes a stronger ability to discern between what is coming from one's own personal feelings and what is coming from intuition.

With practice, you can open your mind and receive intuitive information. However, if your mind is preoccupied with thoughts and feelings, your internal activity can interfere with hearing the data-stream. That would be like a friend who is trying to talk to you from across a crowded room when you don't realize it; they might be talking but you won't notice them. On the other hand, if you understand your friend is trying to talk to you from across a crowded room, you can focus on them so you can understand what they are saying. To go one step further, quiet the room. Then your friend's voice will be much easier to hear, and you will quickly get their message.

Developing your intuition is exactly like this. When you don't know that it's communicating with you, and you are busy with other activities, often you won't even notice it. However, once you have identified that it is trying to communicate with you, you can start to pay attention to it.

The data-stream constantly flows. We only need to recognize it and focus on it. Understand that your thoughts and feelings are like those voices in a crowded room. Learning to quiet the room is absolutely necessary toward developing your intuition. The more you are able to quiet your thoughts and your emotions, the easier it will be to receive your messages clearly, because the more we quiet the room, the better we can hear. People who meditate often have a better connection with their intuition. This isn't because they are necessarily developing a new ability. Rather, they are quieting their mind to hear what's already available to every one of us.

Knowing

Intuition is closely tied to knowing. Knowing comes from developing your intuition and trusting it. We frequently hear people say they trust their gut. When people start to develop their intuition, they often question it, or they are aware that they received some sort of message, but didn't listen to it. Then they experience an unfortunate event, and afterwards say to themselves, "I knew I shouldn't have done that or gone there. Next time I'll trust my gut." Obviously, this is not the optimal way to learn, but it still helps a person to see the accuracy of following their guidance. The more you can see it working for you, the more you will trust it, and the more certainty you will feel. As a formula, it would look like this: Intuition + Trust = Knowing.

When trust in one's intuition is strong, if a horrible catastrophic feeling surfaced, that person would have stopped because he or she KNEW it. Anything we know, we have a definite certainty about. Once you see a scenario play out again and again, where your intuition is validated, you learn to trust that feeling. Eventually, your intuition brings up an instant sense of knowing.

As an example, I worked with "Janey," a woman who visited Florida, where she met a guy I'll call Steve. Steve was from Colorado and Janey was from New York. After returning home, they stayed in touch for more than a year, exchanging emails and phone calls in a long distance relationship.

Steve gave Janey so much attention. She was amazed at what a great guy he was and fell deeply in love with him. At the same time, she felt something wasn't right, but she was so in love with Steve, she pushed those feelings away. She continued their relationship, knowing her intuition was trying to tell her something. Later, she discovered Steve was seeing a lot of women and also married with a family.

If Janey had listened to her intuition and followed it, her outcome would have been different. Janey had the data-stream, but she didn't trust it. Instead, she questioned and ignored it, ultimately suffering the consequences of a broken heart.

Knowing that our data-stream provides valid information for our highest good leads us to have faith in it and confidently make decisions based upon it. Some people say they have faith, but they still hold on to a lot of doubt. True faith is solid and strong. It goes to the level of conviction with a firm expectation that what you sense is accurate.

While it is true that our data-stream can signal danger ahead, we also have to be careful about what we are feeling to make sure it is truly intuition and not a fear coming from our subconscious mind. The programming of our subconscious mind can take over when we step outside our comfort zone. A mixed feeling of fear that originates from our own nervous system or that comes as a result of blocks installed in our subconscious is not intuition. Therefore, if you are facing a big decision, take some time to sit with it and make sure fear isn't interfering with your intuition.

I worked with a client I'll call Antoinette. She was scheduled to be at the Twin Towers on 9/11. As she was preparing to leave that morning, she had an eerie feeling. At first she ignored it, but it got so strong she decided to take the day off and play golf with her husband instead. What a lesson she had that day in trusting her intuition! After that, Antoinette started listening to her intuition more.

Your knowing grows as you flex your intuitive 'muscle' until you fully trust it. As I previously mentioned, when you interact with your intuition by asking about small things — what to eat, how to spend the evening, which people to talk to at an event—you will continue building trust. And with increased trust, your knowing will get stronger.

Healing via the power of the mind

My work involves helping people to heal their bodies and

change their entire lives for the better by using their intuition and the power of their minds. Simply put, our emotions create a physical response in our bodies. An example of this is when someone is embarrassed and their face turns red, or when someone is nervous about giving a speech and ends up with an upset stomach. In my work I have found that all ailments have an emotional link in the subconscious mind. When we release this emotional link, we not only change our health, we change what shows up in our lives, because the subconscious mind controls up to 90 to 95 percent of our actions, behaviors, and what we are attracting.

But there is more to it. For example, if someone feels embarrassed and their face turns red, it will not turn red every time they are embarrassed. There is a reason why a specific reaction in the body occurs, and it has to do with programming held deep in the subconscious. I'll give you an example: One of my clients, who I'll call Jessica, had been experiencing health issues for years. I used my own intuition to ask what emotional link was causing her ailment. In her case, she had stored up resentment. After we identified the emotional link and the issues connected to it, we moved on to release work, which left Jessica feeling lighter and more empowered in her life—plus much healthier as her health issues resolved.

After healing her body, Jessica further developed her own intuition. A few months later, she got a headache and shifted the emotional link to get rid of it. She sent me a text: "OMG! I got rid of a headache on my own. I shifted something and it went away!"

Jessica's fluency in listening to her intuition and understanding what was going on in her body developed into a ability to shift things to make herself feel better. Every human being has this ability; we only need to learn how to access it.

Intuition leads you to your purpose

Connecting to a data-stream from Source energy makes

people feel a deep feeling of connection with others and with the world. It also increases one's sense of safety. With this connection we get clear on our why—our sense of purpose—and our course of action. Frequently, I've witnessed people create great things in their lives because their purpose has become clear as they developed their intuition.

The same is true in my life. After I recovered from that painful illness, I had a knowing that my purpose was to teach people how to heal their bodies, connect their Soul with their intuition, and use the power of the mind to create what they wanted in life.

When I work with people, every area of their lives change—from their health, to their relationships, to their finances, their career, the way they feel, their level of happiness, and their relationship with themselves.

Following my purpose has led me to work with world leaders, CEOs, and celebrities to help them achieve what they want to create in their lives. I've seen people use their minds to change their health in all areas, along with people who are finally able to create the business they want and the level of income they have only dreamed about. To this day I trust and follow my guidance in my own life. Whether I am speaking to one person or an entire audience, my intuition guides me.

From fear to certainty

Reconnecting to our intuition is imperative for life. If a flock of birds stopped listening to what the Universe was saying to them, the survival of the species would be at risk. We, as people, need to reconnect to this feeling of knowing, this intuition, this connection with life and Source.

Many people live in fear, codependency, or uncertainty, and they stress a lot. By connecting with Source, we gain certainty, increase our confidence, and attract healthier relationships. We feel more connection and love for other people from a place of pure joy. We appreciate life.

Our sense of centeredness, certainty, and confidence gives

us power. Coming from that strong foundation, we can then make solid decisions.

What if everyone were able to tap into their guidance system, to live in less fear and worry, and experience a greater sense of safety? What if we always knew we were on the right path? What if there were no more doubts and no sense of dread? Developing your intuition is the key.

Light Practice: Develop your intuition

The best way to develop your intuition is to spend a few minutes each day asking your intuition questions you already know the answer to. By doing this, you will soon identity your brain's method of delivery—whether the information comes to you visually or through your auditory or kinesthetic channels. You will also start to develop a sense of trust. Be sure you are in a relaxed state when doing this exercise. Begin only with "yes" or "no" questions. Ask something as simple as, "Should I have bleach for dinner?" Then focus on what comes up for you. You know you should never have bleach for dinner, so that's an obvious "no." You can use your strong negative response to help you identify exactly how you receive information from your intuition.

Also, ask obvious "yes" questions, such as, "Should I drink water today?" You are not looking for the specific answer; you are identifying the visual, auditory or kinesthetic response that reveals all the answers. As you practice, you will start recognizing the nature of the response and you will connect with it.

Do you have a burning desire to discover the answer to a big question about your life? You can definitely ask a question, such as this. However, if you have a burning desire to know something, you will also have a lot of emotions invested in that situation. Emotions are an energy, which can initially interfere with your ability to hear the response. While you are developing your sense of knowing, it's better to stay with simple questions.

Practice for five minutes a day. Ask questions and listen, using these steps:

- Sit down
- Get in tune with your breathing as it flows through your body
- Get in tune with the way your body feels
- Relax and become present
- Ask obvious "yes" questions
- Ask obvious "no" questions
- Pay attention to the feeling of your response.

You can get information from this invisible source of data just like a computer gets information from the internet. Tapping into your data-stream will set you in a direction that will open you up to more—new levels of awareness, a new path of purpose, or avoiding years of recovery from a bad situation. It can change your life in small ways and large life-changing ways. Continue with this practice until you begin sensing your intuitive response throughout your day. When you do, you will be well on your way to developing your intuition.

People underestimate the importance of their intuition because they haven't taken time to build a trustworthy relationship with it. If they did, they would see how invaluable their intuition is. It can guide them to a more joyous, heartfelt life, and fulfilling their highest purpose.
~Brandy Gillmore

About Brandy Gillmore

After miraculously recovering from a painful health condition and leaving her wheelchair behind, Brandy Gillmore has continued to turn heads by sharing her revolutionary discoveries that changed it all.

She is known for showing people how to make rapid changes to their health and lives in record-breaking time using the power of their own mind with her process called Gillmore Empowerment Technique™ (G.E.T.). Today she coaches celebrities, entrepreneurs, CEOs, and individuals worldwide on her process of "Harnessing Your Inner Power."

Brandy has been featured on stages worldwide and is known for leaving audiences awestruck by demonstrating live results, showing people how to release chronic pain in minutes using only their mind. Her work is frequently described as "miraculous and mind-expanding." She shows people how to truly understand and harness the power of their own minds for healing and transforming their lives.

For more information, *www.brandygillmore.com*

Signs and Synchronicity

By Simran Singh

*God is not a very philosophical concept; it is this world
looked at through the eyes of a child. The same world—
these flowers, these trees, this sky, and you—the same
world takes on a new quality of being Divine when you
look at it through the eyes of a child. God is not missing,
you are missing.*

~Osho

Do you trust life? Do you trust the Universe? Do you trust others? Do you trust yourself? These questions began a series of life experiences that have led to the most amazing and magical conversations with the Universe. But they began in the place that we all find ourselves; those times that are dark, challenged, heavy, and barren. These are the places we do not desire to be in, look at, or experience.

However, those shadow-laden spaces provide the depths and darkness where the Light may sparkle and shimmer all around us, revealing the extraordinary within the ordinary. But in order for this real Light to be recognized, we must be willing to see beyond the illusion of the chaos and challenge that arises. This requires diving into these experiences rather than running from them.

In moments of deep pain, we cry out for help. We ask for signs. While down on bended knee, we pray for guidance. While we prostrate upon the ground, we surrender, in order to bring meaning to life again. In the steps that lead down into this deep abyss of forget-fullness, we hold the hands of skepticism, doubt, and repair. Yet, there is an ever blazing spark within the human spirit; one that fans the flame of hope, wishes, and dreams. It remains alive, flickering within us until we feel the warm remembrance of its call.

Signs are all around us

There are many different ways to live our lives. We can experience the ordinary, seek out the extraordinary, or discover that they are one in the same. There is a tendency to rush past our everyday lives, in search of something shiny in the distance. Sometimes we stop, only to keep looking back for the path that must have been missed. But when we allow ourselves, we become aware of something that catches the eye or the ear. In that moment, we are enamored by a sign, a symbol or a synchronicity. But we believe this is a special occurrence, rare and cosmic. Depending on the state of affairs, many of us ask for another sign to confirm that the first occasion was actually a sign. And at times, even after the second one arises, a third confirmation is wished for.

I have been in many of those same places; questioning, wishing, and wanting. Those were the days I looked for signs and waited for synchronicity. That is what one in fear does; they seek what they can't see. Why? Because they are looking for something beyond what appears right in front of them. And the magic is sitting right before our eyes in every moment. Yes, the signs, symbols, and synchronicities are in front of you all of the time. You have been looking so hard that maybe you have missed them.

What if there truly is only good in the world? And all of that 'good' is there to show you more of you. Is it possible that everything is conspiring to give you messages? Obstacles, challenges, and heartbreak are misconstrued as experiences that tear us down, but what if they are filled with amazing messages that are to awaken us to our Light? What if the signs are so present that every perceived difficulty would resolve if we simply looked more deeply?

My story

I hit that place of rock bottom after years of masked abuse. Ultimately becoming a shell of a person, there was no feeling left inside of me. I was in a complete state of numbness. A moment of surrender came some point after I collapsed on to the floor. In heartbreak and tears, the weight of the world upon my shoulders was only surpassed by the sheer magnitude of self-abandonment, self-denial, and self-betrayal that had been present in my life. In that moment of letting go, I let out a sound, barely a whisper, "Help me God, show me a sign... something... anything..." I did not want to be here anymore. Life was painful; love even more so. I felt alone, angry, stuck, and afraid. I could not fathom that we lived in such a cruel world; that we had a Creator that could stand by and allow suffering. I could not comprehend how or why my life had become what it was.

It was then that the numbers started appearing. I began seeing certain number sequences repeatedly. I was not looking for them, yet my eyes caught sight of them. They would appear in front of me as an address I was to go to, the total on a grocery store purchase, or the license plate sitting in front of me in traffic. They showed up on billboards, buses, and basketball jerseys. They were always flashing back at me on clocks. Once, an entire train passed in front of me with 1111 across each train car.

Some would say this was all coincidence, but is there such a thing? And if there is, then that means time meets matter for a specific date. Would that then be preplanned? Fate? Destiny? Or was something grander at work? Could it possibly be that there are moments of timelessness; not spaces without time. Are there spaces where presence is so profound that awareness is awakened to an underlying pattern of connection between all things? Perhaps synchronicity has nothing to do with time at all, but instead it has to do with us and our degree of presence to be in the moment.

Even then, I remained a bit sleepy-eyed having instances of awareness, and others where I slipped in and out of the chaos of my life. But the signs kept coming. The numbers 11, 111 and 11:11 appeared in my life as many as twenty times a day. I felt as if it were some sort of communication. My mind would chatter that I was crazy. How could the Universe be speaking to me, and of all things, with numbers? But the signs continued.

Finding the meaning

We all want to know what everything means. That was the next place I went. The incessant numbers initially made me feel safe and watched over, as if I had my own special "something" going on. But then they became frustrating. What was the communication? What did it mean? What was the Universe trying to say? The chaos was still present, and now there was confusion as well. In a bout of upset, I demanded to know what it all meant. That is the moment I was handed the next step.

Inspiration took over. Within my mind, I saw these numbers on magazine covers and banners. I had always wanted to be a writer. What appeared before me was a magazine. This was the vision of *11:11 Magazine*.

Without any idea of what I was doing or how I was going to do it, I began by taking small steps. Thirty days later, I had a full issue complete in terms of words but no images and no layout. I realized all of this had began when I had asked for help, so I tried that again. "If I'm supposed to get this magazine out there, bring a graphics person to me. I'm not going to look for one." I shut down my computer, but not before I saw the clock read 11:11.

Blessings in disguise

My computer crashed that night. Forty days worth of work for the new magazine was locked and lost inside. I was shocked that this would be the outcome of so much time and energy.

I called my computer guy who spent several hours trying to fix it. Finally, he was able to extract my last document, 11:11, but I needed a new computer. As I was writing his check, I explained what 11:11 was. He replied, "I know a woman who is an incredible graphic designer, if you need one."

Within this moment of challenge, my computer crashing was a gift. It was the very thing required to open the flow for what I requested. Life was conspiring on my behalf. How else was a graphic designer going to appear on my doorstep?

We often ask for a lot of things but never consider what might have to happen for that very thing to manifest in our lives. Everything in life is always preparing for each new stage to be set. In addition, the symbolism present is humorous and beautiful. My "computer" crashed. I needed a brand new one. The computer is a metaphor for the brain, the body computer. For my life to change, my mind, thoughts, and beliefs had to change. Life was illustrating externally what was now occurring or what needed to occur internally.

Messages in everything

There are messages within every element of every experience. This does not mean we are to drive ourselves crazy trying to decipher each piece and part that unfolds. But it behooves us to be aware of our surroundings, in order to get a general understanding of how the Universe invites us to co-create with it. The Universe can and will use everything in your experience to communicate in, as, through, and with you.

Take time to be aware of what is going on in your home, your car, and your office space. These are all extensions of you to lead and guide you on your way. A flat tire on the right rear of your car is more than the mere illusion of a nail puncture. It is a message that something in the past relating to a male caregiver needs to be addressed because that memory is influencing a current experience, resulting in your being depleted. The right side of your body, vehicle or home is the masculine aspect. The left side is the feminine. The rear of anything is a depiction of the past influence; the front an expression of the future. The objects in life, specifically related to us, are representations of us in various forms to make the game of life more interesting.

Is it crazy? Over the top? Wackadoodle? We do live in a pretty insane world as it is. Is this any crazier than what we see going on in the world? It certainly is more magical, mystical, and fun. It cannot harm anything and supports staying in a mindset and heart-set of support, love, and connection. After all, we create what we believe, consciously and unconsciously. Allow the world outside of you to reflect your unconscious self so you may bring it up to be seen consciously. In doing so, you heal yourself, your life, and your relationships.

Signs appear as everything from personal artwork to children and pets. They also appear as people you meet, words on a card, and a parking space number. These are things that show up in everyday life. They will not be the things you have to look for with a set of binoculars. We are not to scrutinize every little thing in our lives. Instead, we are to be in the natural flow of life, allowing the senses to guide. What does your eye land on when you find yourself fixated on something for no apparent reason? What does your ear hear repeatedly from many sources? What do you find falling into your hands as gifts, books, and symbols? The world is speaking to you, about 'you.' You are having endless conversations all of the time.

Rebel Road Tour

As I moved through the past nine years of my life, I have found that signs, symbols, and synchronicities are anything but random occurrences. They appear in a constant flow throughout the day, speaking paragraphs to each person. In desiring to illustrate this philosophy by example, I decided to embark on an adventure around the country where I only followed the signs. This magical journey was known as 'The Rebel Road Tour.' Over the course of eleven months, there were hundreds of illustrations along the way that clearly show how connected we are to everything.

Upon leaving South Carolina, in September 2013, we stopped for gas about two hours into the journey. The RV would not start when it was time to leave, and we had to get help. Finally, a trucker at the stop jumpstarted us and we were on our way. We arrived in Fayetteville, North Carolina and spent the night. This was our stop on the way to Washington DC where my first event was to take place.

The next morning, we attempted to embark and the RV wouldn't crank up. Eventually a tow truck arrived and we were taken to a nearby 'service' station. As the mechanic tinkered with the RV, other mechanics gathered wanting to know what 'The Rebel Road' stood for. I explained that we each have a unique genius hidden inside and if we follow that spark, we express our individual piece of our Divine puzzle. We each hold a necessary space waiting to be placed. In following the heart's passion, we will naturally be inspired with the answers for the 'problems' in the world. This is the expression of individuality and oneness in harmony.

Upon completing the dialogue, the RV was fixed. The solenoid had to be replaced. The solenoid is a communication device that sits between the ignition and the engine, allowing the message that a key has been inserted and it is time to go. It was the beginning of my journey and I was certain the bill would be six hundred to seven hundred dollars, but instead the mechanic handed me two hundred dollars and a business card. He said one of the gentlemen I had spoken with was the owner. He was inspired by what I was doing and wanted to waive the service fee, donate two hundred dollars, and wish us well. I looked down at the business card and there was a pair of angel wings and the name Jim 'souls.'

We were on our way and reached the RV park in DC. I went inside to get our space and when I came out, the RV would not crank up. Again, I had to be jumpstarted to get to our spot. Once I reached it, I turned off the RV and tried to reignite, and it would not. Having spent the prior several years realizing how connected we are to everything, I knew this was a message, not just a random issue with a vehicle.

I sat back in the RV and asked the Universe to tell me what message it was sending. The first word that popped into my mind was 'solenoid,' pronounced 'sillinoid.' I took a breath and began repeating the word. After the third repetition, it morphed into 'silly noise.' I then got the message. I asked, "Is this how I begin the message of my tour? Is it the 'silly noise' that keeps people stopping and starting, and stopping and starting when it comes to their dreams? If that is the message, please let the RV crank." I went back to the driver's seat, inserted the key, turned the ignition, and the RV cranked up. It cranked for the entire rest of the journey through January 2014.

In this scenario, the RV represents the collective home, illustrating the collective whole. The damaged solenoid was reflective of 'all the chatter inside of our heads,' and 'the chatter of others outside' that keep us moving forward and backing up in life. Needing to be jumpstarted represents the way those outside of us often reignite the spark inside. And this took place on the way to 'our capital,' the place of our 'highest government;' metaphorically the mind.

Getting connected

What if we are all that connected to our reality? What if everything in our external world is merely an extension of our inner world? What if everything is part of the 'play' of the Universe? What if merely changing our thoughts, having an awareness, or staying detached from all experiences, a secret world is revealed that few are aware of? We really do live in a world within a world...within a world.

Life is intended to be magical, playful, and creative. We are here to be children, full of curiosity, wonder, and excitement. The Universe is never going to let us lose sight of that. It is constantly guiding us, sending messages, and having a dialogue. Each and every step, you are not on a journey, you *are* the journey. You are not in the world; you *are* every piece and part of the world. You are experience experiencing itself.

The signs and symbols of your life appear so that you learn to trust. They are ever-present and placed in specific moments and times to aid you where clarity is most required. Coincidences and synchronicity are simply those moments where the authentic you lines up with awareness of the magic moments. You now have the choice to think of that as "special" or "ordinary."

If synchronicity is special for you, then you are still lacking in trust and knowing of your interconnectedness. You would still be in fight or flight, pushing, toiling, and moving against your own grain for the most part. And it will remain a once-in-a-while experience.

If synchronicity is ordinary, then you are living in the flow, recognizing the many pieces and parts of yourself in all the ways that they appear. You have allowed yourself to wipe away the veils from your eyes and ears to see the world as it really is, instead of the way most of us have been conditioned into. In this way, synchronicity will be an everyday experience.

If your life is not working for you, or is not entirely the experience you desire then allow yourself to look at the world in a different way. Things are not as they seem. There are deeper messages in the fabric of life. As you dive in, you will see how interconnected the threads are, which tie each one of us and everything around us together.

Light Practice

Take a moment to reflect on these questions:

Is the Universe having a conversation with you?
Is synchronicity a random occurrence?
Could the obstacles in your life actually hold all the answers?

Is it time to be aware of the ever-present signs, symbols, and synchronicity that surrounds you?

Every person has embedded within themselves a sacred moment when the Soul says 'It's time to turn within and know you are already home.' Each sign, symbol, and synchronicity is a ticking of that clock...until that individual chooses to wake up. There is not one thing in life that does not offer that Truth in the most intensely soulful and personal way.

~**Simran Singh**

About Simran Singh

Simran Singh is publisher of the award–winning *11:11 Magazine* and host of #1 rated, 11:11 Talk Radio. Simran invites people to stand as 'Examples of a New World Paradigm' through creative capacity and authentic living.

Author of *Your Journey to Enlightenment*, *Your Journey to Love*, and IPPY Gold Award Winner of *Conversations with the Universe*, Simran's passionate style takes individuals on a journey into courage, fearless authenticity, and presence.

Spending 30 years in the fashion industry, and the last decade as a voice of Truth in the field of conscious humanitarianism, Simran's writings and 2013 Tedx Talk are real, heartfelt, and connecting because she knows where you are, where you have been, and where you have the possibility of going.

For more information, *www.Simran-Singh.com*

Living Your Purpose

☼

By Kute Blackson

*Not all of us can do great things. But we can do small
things with great love.*

~**Mother Teresa**

Ibelieve we have an individual life purpose in terms of how
our gifts express through us as unique human beings. I feel
that our life's purpose and why we're here is ultimately to
recognize, to remember, and to realign with who we really are.
Every situation, every circumstance, every relationship, no
matter how challenging or confusing, is our teaching. The real
purpose of life is to remember our true essence, that we are
infinite beings, we are Divine, and to live and embody that in
our daily lives as love. It's one thing to remember, 'Wow, this
is who I am. I'm infinite, I'm Divine,' and then just sit on our
couch and bliss out. But because we're in a human body and
not floating in the angelic realms or the higher dimensions,
to me that is a sign we're meant to express who we are in the
world as a form of love.

Part of the reason we incarnate is because there are certain
lessons our Soul is seeking to learn, and certain themes we
need to evolve through and work out on this planet. To me it's
not about being perfect. Some people hold the belief, 'If I heal
myself, and do therapy, and meditate then I'll be this perfect
being.' I don't believe that our purpose is to be a perfect person
who doesn't have any issues, challenges, breakdowns or negative
feelings. As human beings we are here to learn and grow, and
the only way we can do that is through life experiences. When
we awaken to that real deeper purpose of life, then when we
are in the midst of a challenging situation—a breakdown,
a break-up, being broke, getting fired from our job, and so

on, we're able to have a whole different relationship with the situation because we have a different understanding of the real purpose of the type of game we are playing.

In our culture today we forget the game, why we're here, the real purpose of life. We get so identified with our egos, identity, materialism, and acquisition. There's nothing wrong with having a big house and toys…that's a beautiful part of the play of life, but it's also important to think about why are we all here.

When I visited the pyramids in Egypt I saw the Tutankhamen pyramid and where he kept the gold and jewels he had planned to take to the afterlife. Then I visited the Cairo Museum where there was a whole floor dedicated to the Tutankhamen. I saw his throne, his jewels, and his bling…all these possessions he was going to take with him to the afterlife. But he had passed away and his 'stuff' is still here! The truth is, we don't take anything with us when we pass on apart from own Soul's evolution. I feel that life is a Love School. It's great to meditate, elevate into higher dimensions, and astral travel, but the bottom line is that we're in human bodies, and on a practical level the realization needs to lead to our ability to love in human form as a direct experience. Therefore, to me, part of the grander purpose of life is to realize who we are— love—and then to demonstrate that love in our daily lives.

The life purpose myth

I feel that one of the myths we are told in the spiritual and self-help field is that we must know the specifics of our unique life purpose. However, that myth is keeping people stuck and preventing them from moving forward. Some people are teaching that you have to write your life purpose down on a piece of paper and define it. And the students say, "I don't know what my purpose is." However, what if you don't need to know the specifics of your life purpose in order to begin? We all have the ability to feel an inkling. "My Soul lights up around this. I feel moved and inspired around this type of energy, or when I do this activity." There is a part of us that has a sense, but we don't have to get hung up over the form. I tell my clients, "You don't have to know your exact purpose. What's important is to take one step and move in the direction of whatever passion lights you up. Move in the direction that your intuition is guiding you in. You might not know, so embrace the unknown." I believe that life reveals itself to us in the process of living it.

Often we think we know what our life purpose is based on who we are at a particular current state of consciousness. And if we are conditioned, programmed, and not in tune with ourselves then what we think our life purpose is may not be what it truly is. So when you take one step, and then another step, you won't be able to see what's behind that door from five steps behind trying to figure it out. For example, I can almost guarantee that Oprah Winfrey didn't sit back as a 22 year old and say, "I'm going to be the biggest media personality, and have my own cable TV station." But she had a passion to communicate via news and media. She took a step and became a news anchor. She got fired from that role because she was too caring, too emotional, and too passionate. They moved her to a small talk show gig, which no one thought would go anywhere, but it became huge, and one thing led to the next. She simply took a step in the direction of her passions. The reason why most people don't live their life purpose is because they don't take that initial step. One step leads to the next, which leads to the next, then to the next, and all of a sudden you will find that you've *lived into* your life purpose. Living your life purpose starts with the small steps and the trust that life will reveal itself to you as you take action. Through that process we become someone who is more capable of holding the space for the next level of our lives. More gets revealed to us at that time. It takes a greater degree of trust to live this way rather than sitting back and trying to figure everything out. And even if you do supposedly figure out your life purpose, it might not transpire that way. It's always evolving as we evolve. What it is today won't be what it is 15 years from now.

Taking a step

Maybe you say to yourself, 'The only thing that lights me up is music.' Then the mind kicks in and says, 'Yeah, but how am I going to make money with music?' A lot of people say, "My passion is music but I'm going to go and sell cars." That's completely the wrong direction. You might not know exactly how you're going to make money in the music field but if that's what lights you up, follow that impulse and start exploring. Perhaps you make a few phone calls, including to your uncle who's a musician. You get a job, and one thing leads to the next. Then all of a sudden, in five years you're the head of A and R at Universal. It's no different than if you want to go on a vacation to somewhere warm. You don't decide to go to the North Pole. You might decide to go to Hawaii. You don't yet know what island but you get into the vicinity of the Hawaiian islands. And as you hone in you receive clues along the way.

There are a lot of people who tell me, 'Kute, I don't know what my life purpose is.' My advice is, 'Lean into it and see which doors open.' If the doors don't open then maybe that's not it, so course correct. When people don't know what lights them up it's simply their own fear or confusion playing tricks with them. I call it 'the game of confusion.' If we spin that game it allows us to create a smokescreen around ourselves and not risk putting ourselves out there.

I had a client who felt frustrated at not knowing her life purpose. So I asked her what she loved, and her area of expertise. She looked at me and said, "I've been studying autism for 30 years and I can literally help anyone anywhere across the planet with autism." She couldn't believe what she had said, and in a moment of clarity announced, "Oh, I'm an autism expert!" It was right under her nose all along, however she wasn't valuing her skill. Often, if we look at our life experiences, we know our purpose. Perhaps someone has dealt with intense depression or severe addictions so now they have a better understanding of those issues. Our experiences are usually perfectly crafted so we can help other people with those same challenges. Looking at your life experiences is a clue as to how the Universe has been preparing you to do what you're here to do. I believe every experience is a preparation for the next step. It's the Universe's way of cooking you to be able to serve you to the world.

My evolving life purpose

Ever since the age of five, I felt a calling to make a difference. I had a knowing that I was meant to reach a lot of people in my life. My father is a minister, a healer, and a spiritual teacher, who had about three hundred churches in Ghana, and one church in London. When I was eight I started speaking in my Dad's audiences, and profound wisdom started coming out of my mouth. At the age of fourteen I was ordained as a minister, and given a mandate to take over my Dad's churches. However, deep down I felt a discord with that. All I knew was that I was here to make a difference in the world. I started reading spiritual books. Between the ages of eight and seventeen I read about eight-hundred self-help, spiritual, transformational books to try and understand the nature of life. Who are we? Why are we here? Why are some people happy and some people miserable? At the age of seventeen I had an epiphany that my purpose wasn't to take over my father's churches, but rather about helping, inspiring, and awakening people. I came to America with two suitcases after winning a Green Card in a lottery. I tracked down all the most well-known spiritual teachers at the time, such as Jack Canfield and Tony Robbins. I attended their seminars, and sometimes even showed up at their houses and knocked on their doors. Through that I got connected to multi-level marketing, which led me to meeting seminar promoters, and promoting seminars for people such as Les Brown, Jim Rohn, and Tony Robbins. That led to a radio show, which led to speaking and coaching. My life was an evolution. I believe everything that happens is the Universe preparing us for the next step. We often see our vision but maybe we have to grow into that in order to fulfill the intention and the purity of that vision. In my early twenties I had an idea for a TV show and I started tracking down everyone in the industry. I was offered to be represented by the top managers in Hollywood. I was even offered a couple of TV shows at the time but they weren't in total alignment so I declined the offers and went through my own evolution. But last year, twelve years later, I signed a deal for a reality TV show, which is currently in development with one of the largest production companies in the world. Looking back now I thank God that I didn't say yes to the TV show I was offered twelve years ago. Back then I wasn't the same person as I am now. Nowadays I know I can use the platform to make a real difference. We must trust the intelligence and perfection of life and surrender.

The awakening humanity

We are in some of the most amazing times this planet has ever experienced. In Chinese, economic crisis means 'opportunity.' Therefore, we're in the midst of an incredible opportunity as the old systems collapse, such as old economics, old paradigms, old ways of relating, old financial systems, and so on. These no longer work because they're based on fear, greed, separation, and competition. Many of us in that old paradigm may have identified with 'my house,' 'my real estate,' 'my job,' 'my persona,' 'my bank account.' That is now all falling apart, crumbling or shifting in some way. And we're being forced to look deeper. 'If I'm not my house, if I'm not my bank account, if I'm not my persona, then who am I really?' That is the ultimate spiritual question. 'Who am I if

I'm not all I've identified myself to be?'

The world is waking up and through that process we're all being forced to go inside and reconnect. Technology has brought the world together, giving us access to a whole host of information at the click of a button, making the world smaller and facilitating that sense of oneness. Boundaries are dissolving as we're realizing the interconnectedness of us all.

We're alive at this time to participate and co-create in the evolution of the planet. We're evolving as a species to the next level; a group of beings in touch with our Divinity. That consciousness, which Buddha and the Maharishi have been gestating in the Himalayas for so long, is now becoming accessible to us all. What used to be the top of the mountain— reaching enlightenment—is now becoming the bottom of the mountain, the place we all start at. The kids being born today are already enlightened. Each of us taking the responsibility to realize who we really are is how we can all participate in the awakening of humanity.

Light Practice: Connect with your life purpose

Look at your life and your experiences so far. Look at the clues that your life has given you.

What gifts do you have? What are you really good at? If you're still unsure ask a few people around you what they feel your gifts are? If four people say, "You're an amazing communicator and an unbelievable artist" that will point you in a certain direction.

Create the space in your life to be still. Sometimes we're so busy distracting ourselves that we fail to reach that place of stillness inside. When we create the space to be still we can really listen to that inner sense or whisperings of the Soul. This is subtle, so it may only come as an inkling.

Be willing to be honest with yourself. Give up saying, "I don't know." Instead say, "This is my Truth." Own that knowing rather than living in fear. If you don't know what it is then start by reaching out and loving somebody or serving someone.

I believe the form of our life purpose is simply a vehicle to be of service and to be loving. The bottom line is that Love is your purpose.

> *When you stop looking for your life's purpose and start living love as service to those in your life now, magic happens.*
>
> **~Kute Blackson**

About Kute Blackson

Kute Blackson is a unique visionary in the world of human potential. Unlike those who promise to simply help people "get" what they want, Kute's life work instead reveals to people what they have to give, by liberating who they are most truly and deeply. The focus is freedom.

At eight years old, Kute began speaking in front of thousands of people at his father's churches. At fourteen years of age, he was ordained as a minister, given the mandate to take over a spiritual organization spanning three hundred churches. At age 18, through a series of spiritual awakenings, he left everything behind. His entire life has been dedicated to understanding who we are, what we're here for, what makes us truly happy, and how we can achieve our highest potential.

Kute is widely known as a transformational facilitator, speaker, and leader. His inspiring, cutting edge videos have reached millions of people worldwide. He works with clients from all walks of life, ranging from billionaires, celebrities, and entrepreneurs to circus performers, mothers, and children in over 20 countries. Acclaimed worldwide for his transformational experiences, he is considered one of the leading voices in the field of spirituality.

For more information, *www.kuteblackson.com*

Lightworkers and Authenticity

☼

By Rebecca Campbell

I'm not afraid, I was born to do this.
~Joan of Arc

We are rapidly moving into a time in history where anything inauthentic is no longer able to survive. Old methods of patriarchal survival, such as controlling, striving, pushing, sticking at it, and following other people's models of success are not working like they used to. Our lives are being shaken up and anything that is not in alignment with who we truly are, is becoming harder and harder to hold onto. It's as if the rug is being pulled out from so many of our feet in a Universal attempt to rebuild our lives in alignment with who we truly are.

There is an inner Light within each of us that is always calling, ready to guide us home. When we answer its call we are in flow with the Universe. But sometimes it needs to get really dark for us to find it and surrender to its guiding grace.

Finding the Light in the darkness

I have been an avid student of the Soul since picking up my first Mind Body Spirit book when I was fourteen. But in truth I spent almost two decades selectively listening to the calls of my Soul and the path my inner Light was trying to guide me towards. I was attached to patriarchal belief that I needed to make my life happen.

On the outside looking in, my life was great. But increasingly, with every new day, I realized that it wasn't in alignment with who I truly was and who I came here to be. I spent most of my time and energy striving, relying on my own strength, and clinging to things outside of myself to feel loved, valued, purposeful, and successful. It was exhausting and frustrating. The more out of flow with the Universe I got, the harder I tried to hold it all together. I relied too heavily on my masculine energies of making stuff happen rather than leaning into the feminine art of intuitive listening, letting go, and allowing life to support me. Instead of receiving the gifts that the Universe had in store for me I felt like I needed to fight each day to get it. My inner Light was always trying to get my attention, but most of the time I didn't act on it. It took my whole life to come crumbling down, uncontrollable grief, and a whole lot of darkness for me to stop controlling my life and let my inner Light lead.

Within a period of six months the relationship I had been in my whole adult life ended. One of the people I loved most on the entire planet died extremely suddenly. And then another. I woke up to discover that the career I had devoted so much of life to and defined myself by no longer fit my Soul. I moved into a new house and within a week I discovered that even that was falling apart. The irony was not lost on me.

Living in London, away from family and friends back in Sydney, I found myself very far away from home both physically and metaphorically. My foundations had been demolished, and the external things that I clung so tightly to were ripped away.

The blessing: If one of these things had happened on its own, I would have managed to push on through as I had done for so much of my life. However, having so much loss in such a short time, I had no choice but to surrender.

Winter had arrived in the Northern Hemisphere. My loved ones urged me to pack my bags and return to the sunshine in Australia but I had an unshakable knowing that I needed to stay put. I knew that the only person who could get me through this dark night of the Soul for real was me. The life I was born to live depended on it. It was an invitation to venture deep and dark and discover my own inner sunshine.

The Universe had cracked me open, and because of the darkness around me I could make out a small flicker in the deepest caverns of my heart. The more I focused on it, the brighter it got. The brighter it got, the less alone I felt. The more I followed its guidance every day, the more aligned my life became. The more aligned my life became, the more supported by life I discovered I was. The Universe was always waiting to support and cradle me; I was the one who wasn't ready to receive it.

It seems as though this crumbling of foundations is happening to people all over the world right now; a sort of breaking down of the old in order to make way for the new. Our inner worlds and our outer worlds are being shaken back into alignment. The Universe wants us to win. It wants to support us. It wants us to expand alongside it. When we align our lives to our most authentic self, we fall into alignment with the Universe. When we are in alignment with the Universe, life flows and we light up the world just by being in it.

What parts of your life are not in alignment with who you truly are?

What are you clinging to because you're scared that it might disappear with nothing to replace it?

What part of your life and your identity is ready to fall away?

Your inner Light

Your inner Light is your Divine Self. It's your intuition, your authentic spirit, your heart, and your Soul. It's the part of you that led you to read this book and the part of you that just knows. It's part of a greater whole, part of the miraculous web that connects us all. Spirit, Source, Soul, God, the Universe, Grace, Light…whatever name you give it, this mysterious force is calling us every single moment of every single day. It's calling you now and it's going to be calling you tomorrow.

Your inner Light is always calling. *What is your inner Light calling you towards today?*

Your inner Light knows the way

Your Inner Light is always calling you towards your highest path and the most expanded, brightest, joyful, purposeful, fulfilled version of yourself. It's always calling you towards the things that will light you up and make you feel whole. It's always calling you towards the way you can be a bright Light in the world.

Our authentic inner Light speaks to us in feelings, knowing, and intuitive hunches. It whispers in deep yearnings, longings, feelings, and prayers. It doesn't deal in fact and reason or always make logical sense. Listening to it takes courage, answering its call takes balls. The more you follow it, the clearer it gets. The clearer it gets, the easier it is to follow it.

What is your inner Light calling you towards right now?
What is your inner Light calling you away from right now?
If you weren't afraid, what would you do?

Be the Light

A Lightworker is a Soul who knows their Divine nature and answers the call deep within to light up the world with their presence. They know they are here to be a bright Light and devote their life to lighting up the room. Some of us came in with a knowing or memory of this mission, while others come across it through their own awakening process, which is generally spurred on by some sort of cracking open or dark night of the Soul. Lightworkers have one true purpose in life: to be the Light and to serve the world by being themselves.

I have found that what stops so many people from answering this call is a feeling that we might make a mistake. A fear that if we don't choose the right job, modality, gifts, or way of sharing our gifts, we will miss our chance and thus not complete our calling. We place so much emphasis on trying to use our mind to figure out what the heck our calling is, instead of simply following the daily calls of what lights us up.

When we follow what lights us up, we light up the world

without even trying (because we are lit up from following the things that light us up). Our ego is attached to believing that it's more complicated than that. It wants to "work out" the perfect way and slog away in the doing.

But Yogi Bajan didn't say 'do the Light,' he said 'be the Light.' To 'be the Light' we first need to light ourselves up. The surest way to light ourselves up is to follow the things that light us up.

For as long as I can remember I felt a call to devote my life to something bigger—to be a bright Light in the world. However, I felt extremely stressed and weighed down by it all. I knew I was a 'Lightworker' but spent way too much time in inaction, trying to figure out exactly what I was here to do before I let myself start doing it. 'Am I meant to be an actor or an anthropologist? A writer or an artist? A director or a dancer?' Way too many years, drunken conversations, diary entries, and sleepless nights were spent on this pondering.

I tried to work it out as if it was a black and white thing, something that had a final destination, end point, answer, or crystal clear outcome. I was petrified of choosing the wrong thing and thus not fulfilling my calling. I believed I needed to 'find it' like a needle in the haystack. Rather than follow the little calls of what lit me up every single day.

Our inner Light is always leading us towards our gifts. Our inner Light is always saying "Yes," "This way," "Come here," "Do this," "That's right." If you break every decision down, it either strengthens or dims our Light. It either makes us expand or contract. It's either a yes or a no. The Light is always lighting up the path ahead of us; our only job is to follow the trail of things that light us up. What lights one person up will not be the same as the next person. And so by following the trail, we come to light up our corner of the world in a way that only we can.

What lights you up?

Just like a moth to a lamp, when we say "yes" to the things that light us up, the Universe bends to support us. Our life begins to align and we start dancing with the Universe. Before long, we find ourselves right in the center of our passion, wondering why it took us so long to find it in the first place.

When you follow the things that light you up, don't be attached to the outcome or feel the need to do it for an end result. Simply do them for the joy, the feeling, for the love of it. So if writing lights you up, don't write to get published, write because you love writing. Show up every day and lose yourself in the writing.

It doesn't matter if it's ten minutes or ten hours. If you only have ten minutes a day to devote to it, then show up for ten minutes every day. After a year those 3560 minutes will likely roll into some unexpected creation or open some new door that had you not shown up would not have been possible. If you get published, then that is a bonus. But the fact is, it does not matter if you get published, for you will be lighting up the world just by showing up to your keyboard each day. It's not about the outcome or the end goal; it's about the daily act.

So if you love creating art, create something beautiful. If you love walking on the beach, walk on the beach. If you love creating order, organize. If you adore traveling, travel. If you love driving, drive. If cooking lights you up, cook. If your heart swells each time you see flowers, buy some for yourself today. Do the things that light you up and you will light up the world in an instant. The more you do them, the more one thing will lead to another and you will discover your own way of doing them. As you show up to the things that light you up, ideas will land in your lap. You could incorporate your love for flowers with your adoration for travel. Had you not shown up to those two things, you might not have been in a state to receive the idea in the first place. The end result does not matter; all that matters is that you show up to the things that light you up.

When we lose ourselves in the doing, something magical happens. We get our ego out of the way and allow the Light to stream through us. It's why we feel like we could do it for hours upon hours. We find a space of bliss. When we are in this space we allow ourselves to be filled up, and we also light up our part of the world. When we let the Light shine through our unique beings we harmonize the planet in our own authentic way.

Light Practice

What lights you up? What makes you expand? What opens your heart? What puts a smile on your face? What are you enthusiastic about? What do you love doing?

1.
2.
3.
4.
5.
6.
7.
8.
9.
10.

Work your Light

If you follow what lights you up, you will light up the world in a way that only you can, because there is no other being quite like you in the Universe.

Your Soul has been colored and shaped by experiences from all of your lifetimes. In fact, there is no other Soul in the history of souls who has had the same experiences as you. There is also no human in the history of all human beings who has had the same experiences as you. When you put these two things together, it's crazy that we try to be like one another.

There is no being in the history of all beings who has the same way of seeing things, feeling things, understanding things, creating things, saying things, singing things, drawing things, writing things, wearing things, painting things, explaining things, hearing things, laughing at things, pondering things, expressing things. Therefore, the way you shine your Light will be completely different to how someone else shines theirs.

Our inner Light is the part of us that is connected to everything and everyone. It has been there from the moment we were born, and it can never be extinguished. We all have an inner Light but it is not of us, rather it is part of the larger mysterious Divine Light Source that is waiting to shine through each and every one of us. As it shines through our uniqueness, it creates the most magical light show.

When you resist all that you are (or try to be more like someone else), you dim your Light and block the Light (Source) from flowing through you. We are not meant to be the same carbon copies or perfect beings. Perfection does not exist. Rather, it is through embracing our imperfection that true perfection is born. When we embrace all that we are, we act as clear channels and give the Light a clear channel to shine through. When we allow the Light to shine through us we light up the world in a way that only we can.

We are each like intricate stain glassed windows. When we let the Light shine through us, the most breathtakingly beautiful creations are effortlessly created. If you have two singers, the Light that shines through each of them and their creations will be completely unique. Let's call an end to competition. For as we all shine our unique Light in our own unique way, we bring both beauty and harmony to the planet. And right now, the planet needs it more than ever.

If it's in your heart, it's your path

If you have a dream, a vision, and an urge to create, trust the seed that longs to sprout and give it everything it needs. We all have dreams, visions, and creations that are yearning to be born. Some were planted even before we were born, tugging at our Soul strings to give them what they need to grow.

Nurture them with all of the Light you can fathom. Protect them and give them enough space to thrive. Drench them with baby steps and encouragement every single day. Invest in them with your time and attention. Walk them forward with every ounce of courage you can conjure. Just show up. Everyday show up. And let your inner Light illuminate the way.

Any creation that is born in the Light of your heart is a creation calling to be born. If you let this creation flow through you, that creation will light up the world. Don't keep these creations locked away. They are there for a reason. Take a thousand deep breaths if you need to and let the birthing process do its thing. It knows what to do.

Light Practice

What creations or dreams want to be born into this world by you?

1.
2.
3.

How can you show up to them today?

1.
2.
3.

Follow what lights you up and you'll light up the world.
~**Rebecca Campbell**

About Rebecca Campbell

Rebecca Campbell is a bestselling author of *Light Is The New Black* and *Rise Sister Rise*, published by Hay House, an inspirational speaker, grounded spiritual teacher, and intuitive guide. Through her soulful writing, creations, and teachings she has guided thousands of people to listen to the callings of their Soul and live the life they were born to live.

Rebecca teaches internationally and is passionate about helping people live a life that is in alignment with their Soul.

Rebecca was awarded 'Best Emerging Voice' by *Kindred Spirit Magazine* and 'Promising New Talent' by the Mind Body Spirit Festival. She believes that when we follow what lights us up and courageously share that with the world, we light up the world with our presence. Prior to stepping out of the spiritual closet, Rebecca enjoyed a successful career as an award winning Creative Director in advertising, where she helped some of the world's most recognized brands find their authentic voice.

Originally from the sunny shores of Sydney, Rebecca now lives in London but you can find her down under most summers getting her salt water and sunshine fix.

For more information, *www.rebeccacampbell.me*

The Incredible
Lightness of Being

☼

By Julie Chimes

Thy priests go forth at dawn;
they wash their hearts with laughter.
~Egyptian Book of the Dead

I have always loved this saying from the ancient Egyptian Book of the Dead—how delicious it sounds to wash one's heart with laughter. When I was a very small child I would sit in the wings of London's West End and watch hundreds of people enter the theater with all their rustling, jostling, and coughing. The cacophony of sound would settle into hushed expectation as the lights went down and a single spotlight splashed a bright yellow blob on the stage. I used to tremble, picking up a deep sense of backstage terror as my famous stepfather would step out of the darkened wings into that light—it seemed an impossible career that he had chosen. He was paid to make people laugh. Yet from the first moment he stepped onto the stage he created a ripple of delight. I observed this lone man, fascinated as he talked to his audience as he would his closest friends, gaining their trust as he delivered his laconic observations of everyday life. The sounds of chuckles, giggles, and guffaws grew into a roaring force that would, with his masterful timing, eventually explode into laughter. It was a marvelous sensation to sit and feel all of that energy, which literally shook the very foundations of the building. I guess you could say I felt the good vibes. All my fears would melt away and I would revel in the wonderful atmosphere of happiness that magically seemed to permeate everyone and everything in the building!

As with many famous comedians, there was a dark side to my surrogate father's nature. Often after shows his mood would plummet and a cruel monster would somehow take a hold of him, and systematically this inner demon would try to destroy everything in its path, including my mother, my brother, and me. I remember one night being locked in the kitchen and hiding behind curtains, my mom holding a huge pan aloft ready to protect her terrified babies. In a different take on The Shining, my stepfather actually jumped through the door, screaming and ranting with the full force of madness. As he ripped the curtain from its pole revealing his terrified family, something unexpected happened. My mother started to laugh. She laughed so much she was crying and I had to laugh too as it was so infectious. Then my brother joined in and all the fulminating rage and threat of violence evaporated into the night air.

So you see, my love affair with laughter began at an early age. I knew, even then, that there was a mystical quality about true, belly-shaking joy. There was no need for analysis as it was obvious to my infant mind that this was a power that produced miraculous results. Now, many decades later, the UK's Oxford University scientists have proved something the mystics have been telling us for centuries—that laughter is good for us.

A merry heart doeth good like a medicine.
~**Proverbs 17:22**

And that does not mean polite titters, but rather the experience of uncontrolled mirth that leaves us exhausted, triggering the release of protective endorphins. These endorphins, one of the complex neuropeptide chemicals produced in the brain, manage pain and promote feelings of health, happiness, and an incredible lightness of being. The boffins also tell us we are 30 times more likely to trigger this state of blissed-out wonder, if we share the experience with others. Psychologist Jack Panksepp proved this in his experiments with animals. Want to see a rat laugh? Then tickle it. Rats laugh, chimps laugh, and so do dogs, but they aren't laughing at jokes. They laugh when they're playing, in the same way humans do, to show that they're happy and to encourage bonding. The rats that played more, laughed more. And the ones that laughed more preferred to be around other rats that laughed. There is something inherently infectious about surrendering to joy. Try being around a chuckling baby or a 'grinning' playful animal and remain serious—it's impossible! In all the thousands of languages and means of communicating that exist, the expression of laughter is Universal. Every being upon this Earth has a primordial knowing of how to express mirth and happiness. Research suggests that as babies we laugh a great deal of the time, and yet in most, this diminishes as we grow up. We seem to have buried the connection to our ecstatic essence under the silt of wrong-identification and a heavy sense of duty and doership.

The standard dictionary definition of lighthearted is joyful, glad, taking pleasure in being alive. Not depressed or sad. Enjoyable lack of seriousness, not grave.

Laughter holds the key to that extraordinary state of lightheartedness. In these various studies of infants and animals it is clear that they laugh a lot more than adults, delighting in simple fun and games. I am convinced we all have a hidden chuckle muscle hidden in the vocal chords and it needs exercising every day. I've always felt that youthfulness and vocal versatility is directly linked to our ability to be happy. My autistic brother, Martin, tells me that when we laugh we 'go all sparkly round our heads.' Our mother had an outrageous sense of fun and she remained a stunningly beautiful woman until she became unable to forgive something. The first thing she lost was her ability to sing. The chuckle muscle wasted away and she lost her vitality and joy, becoming a sad and bitter woman, which reflected in her face. Sadly, she faded away and left this Earth in a pool of tears and pain. I miss her very much, especially her ability to make me laugh. The sound of her mirth would always set me off too, utterly infectious, highly inappropriate, I was most often rendered helpless into a weeping, shaking heap. As the old joke goes, Sometimes I laughed so hard the tears ran down my leg.

> *Among those whom I like or admire, I can find no*
> *common denominator, but among those whom I love,*
> *I can; all of them make me laugh.*
> ~W.H. Auden

So, what is it that stifles and suppresses our natural lightness of heart? The sages and mystics and the scriptures of Truth teach us that our true nature is full of fun. They also teach that the enemy of joy, laughter, and the incredible Lightness of Being is when the ego gets involved. For the ego is the sworn enemy of Lightheartedness. They tell us that a sense of humor and delicious laughter is a sign of Divinity. Perhaps this is why there are so many laughing Buddhas? Is this the Divine Comedy—that when one breaks free from the veils and sticky, heavy layers of ego, we are able to express our wonder and amusement at all things, even the difficulties and tragedies?

I once experienced an intensely difficult piece of human karma, when I was stabbed repeatedly by a paranoid schizophrenic on a mission to save the world in the name of Jesus. As both the world and I remain I'm unsure as to the success of her mission but I did discover a few very interesting things, which helped me rediscover my connection with the Divine Comedy. In fact, when I wrote of my experience being on the receiving end of psychotic violence and the subsequent adventures on the other side of the door marked death, do you know what readers and audiences were most shocked by? Not the size of the knife, the number of injuries and stitches, or the fact my assailant was a woman. No, the shock factor was that not only could I forgive but I could also laugh and joke about being almost murdered. That knife somehow punctured far more than my body—it also managed to rip through those layers of ego until I discovered what was within me, and that discovery held the key to one of life's greatest mysteries and paradoxes. As the Buddhists say, "One I wept and the other laughed."

In those moments of experiencing my death, I knew with all of my being that taking life seriously or personally was probably the most ridiculous and spiritually immature stunt a human could take.

I was in an altered state of consciousness and exploding with feelings of joy whilst at the same time tears of compassion rolled down my face for my assailants.

The ancient language of Sanskrit defines it better than anything else I have discovered.

Sat Chit Ananda - The true knowledge and awareness of The Self, as Consciousness, is Bliss.

Yet, we run away from our true nature, instead of being taught to go within. We spend much of our time looking outside of ourselves to feed and satisfy the senses, hoping something out there in the big wide world will come along and make us happy again. The right partner, home, country, bank balance, job, car, friends, holidays, blah blah blah.... Even some of the supposedly 'spiritual books' get us to focus and visualize on attaining outer things as some sort of measure of success. Yet we can never be defined by what we own. It is simply our karma and a perfect design to help us to ask the right questions to hopefully turn our attention back within. In my darkest hour I was blessed to receive wisdom from a wise-cracking being whom I nicknamed Veritas. I suppose I could say that Veritas was my guardian angel, waiting to guide me through the attempted murder, but this being was nothing like an angel of religious art or imagery and certainly was not going to let me take anything seriously. I had many discourses and arguments with the enigmatic Veritas until gradually I began to see life with much more of an overview and with far less need to take anything personally.

Me - Am I dead?

Veritas - From my perspective you have never been more alive.

Me - But I am lying in that driveway full of stab wounds, so who is this watching the event?

Veritas - Indeed, asking who you are is a great question. Clearly you are far more than that body in the driveway, which was the vehicle you chose to drive around in…and by the way, it is not the write-off you imagine although I admit the crash damage is pretty extensive.

Me - I'm not going back into that smashed body. It's all so unfair. I haven't even begun to live.

Veritas - It's a perfect design. No punishment intended, simply an act of love created to bring you to your true home. From where I stand it's Bliss. You are watching a film where ultimately no one dies and no one suffers. All of the actors signed a contract beforehand, including you. Lighten up my friend and enjoy the play.

In the presence of Veritas it was impossible to be a 'poor little me.' I became so elated in this presence of such immense Light that I began to feel myself dancing with joy in a realm of complete love, laughter, and freedom. I experienced that incredible Lightness of Being and a peace that truly surpassed all understanding. Even now, many years later, I can still feel the bubbling up of pure delight and the deepest love and gratitude for everything life has thrown my way. I still experience many adventures in the realms beyond the physical body, and I can report back that the nature of everyone on this planet is love, cheerfulness, and bliss. Life is the ultimate game of hide and seek, and it takes grace, courage, and dedication to reveal this Truth.

Our lightheartedness diminishes when our search for

happiness pulls us deeper and deeper into the material world; a world that can never satisfy the yearning to know who we really are. Unless we have some sort of spiritual awakening, we become caught in the melodramas, darkness, and emptiness of the illusion, and become vulnerable to the negativities, which of course leave us in a state of heaviness, where it is almost impossible to express laughter or joy. Egoic humor becomes cruel, sarcastic, bitter, and punitive.

TRIPPING OVER JOY
What is the difference
Between your experience of Existence
And that of a saint?
The saint knows
That the spiritual path
Is a sublime chess game with God
And that the Beloved
Has just made such a Fantastic Move
That the saint is now continually
Tripping over Joy
And bursting out in Laughter
And saying, "I Surrender!"
Whereas, my dear,
I am afraid you still think
You have a thousand serious moves.
Hafiz, *I Heard God Laughing*

So, perhaps we should take a joyful peep behind the egoic mask of misery to reveal why so much of humanity has lost the ability to be cheerful?

The infant daughter of a friend of mine loves pretending to be a grown-up. There is something so heart-meltingly cute about the way she teeters around in the big shoes, telling everyone what to do! What's not so charming is the way her facial expression goes from dimpled joy into one of scowling, disapproving, dour concentration. Is this what we look like as become grown-ups? Travelling in a London rush hour recently I realized that sadly, most adults do wear a mask of grim-faced, tight-lipped seriousness. Smiling is treated with utmost suspicion and tends to denote a tourist or bumpkin from 'out of town.' It is often not considered sophisticated or cool to be happy. Ironically, access to news and friendship via technology and social media have added to the seriousness, producing one of the most anti-social generations this planet has ever known. Have you ever tried speaking with someone who has their focus on a mobile device or computer? They are not fully present and only give a fraction of their attention to that which lies beyond their screen. Therefore, they miss the warmth of human exchange and have cut themselves off from the Source of Joy. It is not possible to experience the Bliss of Being if one is not fully present in the moment. Sometimes it takes a 'head-on karmic crash' to get the purpose of life back into perspective.

We have wrongly identified ourselves as human doings
rather than human beings.

The egoic layers that cut us off from our Truth are complex and constitute the enemy that needs to be tackled. In mythology and sacred texts the warrior has to face many tests and challenges before he or she can win the treasure, the ultimate goal of human existence, enlightenment. We cannot run away forever, and for every life there is a turning point when we have to face ourselves with honesty. When the spiritual warrior within us arises, life can never be the same again. A sacred battle commences between what I call Igor, the Ignorant ego, and our higher Truth. Igor demands be taken seriously, and laments 'without me nothing would happen.' Igor is inhibited often as extroverted, poor little me, life is not fair, or struts around demanding attention. Igor has to be right about everything and the word 'humility' does not form a part of its vocabulary unless prefixed by the word false. Igor never laughs unless it is at someone else's expense. I always know when my ego has flared up as I feel heavy-hearted and a sense of hopelessness. It really does need whacking over the head with a large pan—and in Truth this is what any authentic Master or teacher will do to us. Because out of their immense compassion, love, and knowing, they understand that removing the veils will reveal our true nature, our Light, and then the wellspring of inner joy will bubble up into our lives, infusing us with the incredible Lightness of Being. Life then becomes intuitively obvious and we are guided to bring forth our talents and gifts and share them for the betterment of humanity. We realize that being of service to the Divine is the best game in town.

Much of our modern world has forgotten how to encourage playfulness. There is so much pressure on everyone. Children are expected to perform, even at pre-school, homework has increased, and playtime, music, dance, and creativity take second place to academic achievement. How many governments invest in the happiness of their people? Bhutan is probably the only country in the world that measures and assesses the gross national happiness of its populace. This measure of quality of life or social progress in more holistic and psychological terms is recognized as more important than the Gross Domestic Product (GDP).

A modern saint recently said that an enlightened country and government will place the happiness of its people at the top of any agenda. Those with money are encouraged to become patrons of the Arts, and supporters of projects that encourage all aspects of creativity, beautiful architecture, nature being honored, parks, gardens, space, and peace. Art, dance, literature, and music play a central role in the upliftment of humanity, and humor is always present in an awakened society. We have to learn to laugh at ourselves and comedians do a marvelous job in helping us find mirth in the midst of the madness. I will always thank my troubled genius of a stepfather for helping me see the world through his comedic eyes. The saint went on to say that one night of uplifting entertainment has the power to change a nation. I found that statement profound. We have the power to change communities and kingdoms when we present works that uplift, unite, and amuse.

With mirth and laughter let old wrinkles come.
~**William Shakespeare**

Let's grow old together with laughter in our hearts. Let's accept our earthly duties, Dharma, with a sense of joy and enthusiasm. Let's be kind to one another. Let's really make a difference to this world by spreading our delight and sharing our laughter, as friends of old. May our youthful spirits learn to treat this life as if it were a trip to a great movie or play. May we learn to be the witness and enjoy being a player on the Universal stage of the Divine Comedy. As my beautiful brother Martin said, "May we make our precious world much brighter and happier when we go all 'sparkly around our heads.'" May we all come to know the incredible Lightness of Being and rest in our true nature.

Lighten up my friends. This world could do with a little more sparkle. Remember that a smile can travel faster and further than a frown. Good humor and fun is the best game in town. When you find the source of your mirth you will know the purpose of human birth. In laughter we will merge into the arms of the Divine, where we will discover we are all born to shine.
~**Julie Chimes**

About Julie Chimes

The conventional world of Julie Chimes underwent a dramatic change when an out-of-the-blue attempt on her life left her for dead. Viciously stabbed repeatedly within millimeters of her life her subsequent survival was considered to be something of a miracle. She wrote a profound, yet humorous autobiographical account of her experiences both in and out of body, *A Stranger in Paradise*, published by Bloomsbury, London. The story has always created positive media attention, and as a result, with humor and compassion, Julie shares her inner and outer adventures with diverse audiences around the world.

Julie is currently working on a musical version of her experiences with kindred spirit Russell Nash. Both passionate about finding Veritas, the authentic voice of one's Highest Truth, their music, performance, retreats, and master classes encourage and empower others to experience the Incredible Lightness of Being within, the abode of Unconditional Love.

For more information, *www.juliechimes.com*

Section 2

The traveler had hiked a long distance, and he felt hot and sweaty, exhausted from his journey so far. Now on the coast, he sat upon a giant rock and stared out to sea, allowing his thoughts to ebb and flow with the tide, while his body cooled down.

Suddenly, his head turned to the left and he found himself looking directly at the lighthouse. A ray of golden light shone down from it, as if speaking to him and only him. At that precise moment, three white butterflies landed on his backpack, and he received a strong inner knowing that it was time to continue his journey.

We Are All One

By Patricia Cota-Robles

> *If you are driving home from work and your gaze is caught by a glowing sunset, consider that nature wanted to catch your attention, not that you and the sunset are having just an accidental encounter. On some intimate level, your existence meshes with the Universe, not by chance but by intention.*
>
> **~Deepak Chopra**

The Light of God is increasing on Earth. This is due to myriad activities of Light that have been co-created over the past several decades through the unified efforts of embodied Lightworkers and the beings of Light in the realms of illumined Truth. This influx of Light is causing a shift of consciousness and an awakening within the hearts and minds of people everywhere. These awakening souls are beginning to "see with new eyes and hear with new ears." From the very depths of their hearts they are asking the questions, "Who am I? Why am I here?"

One of the most significant responses that humanity is receiving from the realms of illumined Truth is that we are one with every particle and wave of life throughout the whole of creation. That means that separation and duality are illusions. There is no such thing as "us and them." We are all interconnected, interrelated, and interdependent, not just with each other, but with the nature kingdom, the Earth, and the cosmos.

The statement "we are One" has been reverberating through the ethers since the beginning of time, but it has usually been discounted as a lofty platitude or religious rhetoric. In reality, that statement reflects a profound Truth that includes every atomic and subatomic particle and wave of life that has ever existed or will ever exist in any time frame or dimension, both known and unknown.

From the time we were first breathed into manifestation as individualized sons and daughters by our Father-Mother God, we were invested with the creative faculties of thought and feeling. We were also given the gift of freewill, so we could choose what we wanted to create through our thoughts and feelings. Since our inception, every thought or feeling we have ever expressed has either added to the Light of the world or the shadows, depending on what our frame of mind and our emotional state of being was at the time.

Creative thoughts

At any given moment our life experiences are reflecting the sum total of what we have created with our thoughts and feelings throughout our earthly experiences. This is true whether our creations, or miscreations, were created deliberately or inadvertently. It is also true that whatever we have created is not only affecting us; our creations and our miscreations are affecting all life everywhere, because we are One and there is no separation.

We are not the victims of circumstance. We are the co-creators of the circumstances taking place in our lives. What is occurring in our everyday life experiences is the result of how we have used our life force and what we have chosen to empower with our thoughts and feelings throughout our entire earthly sojourn.

This information is not being given to humanity by the Company of Heaven to instill guilt or feelings of failure consciousness within us. That is a major part of our problem already. For millennia the various world religions have programmed into us the grossly inaccurate information that we are "worthless sinners and worms in the dust." Since our thoughts and feelings are creative, and since we become who we believe we are, it is no wonder that the masses of humanity are floundering in the oppressive grip of our fear-based human egos.

We are being reminded of these profound Truths so that we will once again know that we are not the victims of our lives; we are the co-creators of our lives. If we do not like what is happening in our lives or in the world, we have the ability to do something about it by empowering our thoughts, feelings, words, actions, and beliefs with what we want to experience, instead of the pain and suffering we may be experiencing now.

Amazing beings

As you read the following information that has been given to us from On High, center yourself in the divinity of your Heart Flame. Allow the following words to awaken within you the inner knowing and the remembrance of who you really are, and the fact that you are One with all of life. As this Truth resonates in the deepest recesses of your heart, you will know beyond a shadow of a doubt that you are not the fragmented, fear-based aspect of your personality known as the human ego. You are an empowered and deeply loved child of God.

In Truth, you are a magnificent, multifaceted, multidimensional reflection of our Father-Mother God, and all that our God parents have is yours. Your God Self, which is your I Am presence, is a radiant sun expressing all of the various frequencies of divinity pulsating in the causal body of God. This is a cosmic moment on Planet Earth and you are here for a reason. You are a beloved son or daughter of God participating in the greatest leap in consciousness ever experienced in any system of worlds. You are a powerful instrument of God, and together with Lightworkers all over the world, you are co-creating a new Earth and a new octave of Godhood. Your Light is now expanding the infinite body of God without measure, and you are lifting every particle and wave of life ever breathed forth from the core of creation into the dawn of a new cosmic day.

You may not realize this Truth yet, but you are a wondrous gift to this planet, and all life evolving here is blessed by your presence. Now, from this level of understanding, let us proceed.

Our oneness

What we call "God" is the omnipotent, omniscient, omnipresent, and all-encompassing luminous presence of divinity that envelopes all life everywhere. This includes every minute electron, atom, subatomic particle, and wave of life evolving in any time frame or dimension throughout infinity. God is the cosmic I Am, All That Is. What that means, both literally and tangibly, is that everything that exists anywhere in the whole of creation is a "cell" in the body of God, or what science is beginning to call the Divine Matrix.

Knowing that, we can then understand that all life forms live, move, breathe, and have their being within the Divine Matrix of our Father-Mother God. Therefore, what affects one part of life affects all life. What affects one "cell" has an effect on all of the "cells" in the body of God.

This is the reality of our oneness. Every single thing we do affects the whole body of God. Every thought, feeling, word, or action we express changes the dynamics of the entire Universe. There is no such thing as neutral energy. At any given moment, depending on our frame of mind and our emotional state, we are either adding to the collective Light of the world or adding to the shadows. How is that for an awesome responsibility?

So why do things seem to be getting worse day by day? Because the Light of God is increasing on Earth! It is very important for us to really understand this phenomenon, so that we will be able to see the bigger picture and not allow ourselves to be overwhelmed with feelings of fear or hopelessness when we observe the events taking place on the planet.

The Light of God

As the Light of God flows into the physical plane through humanity's newly awakened hearts and minds, it pierces into the spark of divinity pulsating within the core of purity in every atomic and subatomic particle and wave of life evolving on Earth. As the Light penetrates into the Divine spark in every electron of life, it reactivates the immaculate concept that is encoded there. The immaculate concept for any of God's creations is the blueprint for that expression of life's full Divine potential. The reactivation of the immaculate concept is happening within all life on this planet at this time. This is true whether we are talking about a person, a place, a condition, or a thing, or whether we are referring to the human kingdom, the elemental kingdom, or the angelic kingdom.

No matter how distorted or mutated a life form is, its very core still pulsates with the spark of Divinity and the immaculate concept for its original Divine potential. Without that, no life form can survive. In other words, even within the most depraved or degenerate Soul there still blazes a spark of divinity with all of the Divine potential of a son or daughter of God, or that Soul could not exist. This is a vitally important point for us to comprehend. Once we really grasp this Truth, it will change the way we look at life and how we feel about people in general.

Within the core of every negative situation or manifestation on Earth, the original Divine potential also exists. Within every electron of poverty still pulsates the potential of God's limitless abundance. Within every electron of disease still pulsates the potential for vibrant health. Within every electron of war still pulsates the potential of eternal peace. Within every electron of hate still pulsates the potential of God's infinite love.

What is happening on the planet now is that the Light of God is flowing into the Earth at an accelerated pace through the Heart Flames of awakening humanity. This influx of Light is activating the immaculate concept of the original Divine potential within the core of every person, place, condition, or thing on Earth. This phenomenon is pushing every frequency of energy, vibration, and consciousness that conflicts with the Divine potential of that person, place, condition or thing to the surface to be healed and transmuted back into Light.

Negativity in the Light

The reason things look so dire from outer appearances is because it is very easy for humanity to witness the negativity being pushed to the surface all over the world. What is much more difficult is for the masses of humanity to see the incredible Light of God that is pushing that mis-qualified energy to the surface. Therefore, from our limited perspective it looks like things are getting worse, but that is an illusion and nothing could be farther from the Truth. I assure you, our Father-Mother God would not be allowing this intensified cleansing to take place if it was going to cause more harm than good.

As the frequencies of energy that conflict with the Light of God surface in each of our lives, we respond to them in various and sundry ways. For example, the frequencies being pushed to the surface that conflict with Divine Love are hatred, fear, jealousy, resentment, low self-esteem, envy, intolerance, prejudice, greed, selfishness, indifference, lack of compassion, disrespect, and other emotions that reflect a lack of reverence for life. If we look at that one aspect of our Divine potential and observe the negative effects of the energies being pushed to the surface that conflict with Divine Love, we will clearly see why things seem so bleak on Earth.

As these negative patterns surface, people who don't understand about the oneness of life often latch on to the distorted patterns and act them out in their daily lives. That is why we are seeing a tremendous increase in hate crimes, ethnic cleansing, war, prejudice, intolerance, corruption, discrimination, road rage, physical abuse, dysfunctional families, violence, shootings, drug abuse, abuse of the Earth, and all manner of disharmony and imbalance. From outer appearances it looks as if the world has gone amuck. That is why this time was referred to in the Bible as, "the time of screaming and the gnashing of teeth." Does anybody have any doubt about that?

It is certainly not the intent of our Father-Mother God for

the increased influx of Light to take us down the tubes. In fact, if there was even the slightest potential of that happening, the present level of cleansing would not be occurring.

Purpose of Lightworkers

All of us have been preparing for eons of time to assist during this unique moment on Earth. Our responsibility as Lightworkers is to daily and hourly use our creative faculties of thought and feeling to add to the Light of the world. With every thought, feeling, word, or action we express during the day we should ask ourselves, "In this moment, am I adding to the Light of the world or the shadows?" If we are not adding to the Light of the world, we need to say to ourselves, "How can I change the way I am thinking, feeling, speaking, or acting in this situation in order to add to the Light of the world? How can I react to, or solve, this problem in a positive way?"

By quieting ourselves, taking a deep breath, and asking our I Am presence for guidance, we will begin to perceive other ways of responding. Then we can go into action and deliberately do whatever is necessary to improve the way we are handling the situation. We do not have control over the things from our previous behavior patterns that are returning to us, both individually and collectively as the family of humanity, to be healed and transmuted back into Light. We do, however, have absolute control over how we allow them to affect us and how we respond to them.

Once we have mastered this ability, which is not too difficult with consistent practice, we can share what we have learned with our families, our loved ones, and the people in our spheres of influence. This does not mean judging people, getting on our soapbox, or preaching to them. It means giving people a drink from our cup of knowledge once they have asked and indicated that they are ready to receive it.

The effects of our experiences and our sharing will be exponential. Step by step, we will educate the masses of humanity and help people remember the oneness of all life.

Through this process people will learn that when we hate anyone it is the same as hating ourselves. When we are prejudice or discriminate against someone because of the color of his or her skin, religion, nationality, culture, gender, life-style, economic or social status it is the same as hating ourselves.

Remember, every particle and wave of life in the whole of creation is a cell in the body of God. Every thought, feeling, word, or action we express affects every part of life and changes the dynamics of the Universe. All of the "cells" in the body of God have unique gifts, purposes, and reasons for being just like the cells in our own bodies. We have a multitude of cells in our physical bodies that serve various functions, all for the good of the whole. To say that we hate people because they are different than we are is like saying, "I like heart cells, but I hate stomach cells and lung cells." The heart cannot survive without the stomach and the lungs. These organs need to function in harmony with each other in order for the body to survive and be healthy. All cells are important! Their diversity is vital and necessary. Can you envision what a different world this will be when we comprehend the magnitude of the profound Truth that we are all One and that we are all vital and necessary for the harmonious function of the entire body of God? We must remember that harming another part of life is like shooting ourselves in the foot and that only when every single person on Earth is loved, cared for, nurtured, and valued, will we be truly happy, fulfilled, and living in God's eternal peace and limitless abundance.

Light Practice: Magnetizing the patterns of perfection for the New Earth through humanity's heart flames

In order for patterns of perfection for the New Earth to manifest in the physical plane, the Company of Heaven needs our help. In alignment with Universal Law, the call for assistance must come from the realm where the assistance is needed. In order for these life-transforming patterns to manifest in the physical plane of Earth, they must be drawn through the Heart Flames of people abiding in the physical plane. Even though the Company of Heaven is assisting us in every way possible, unless the patterns of perfection for the New Earth are invoked into the physical plane through the Heart Flames of embodied Lightworkers, they will not tangibly manifest on Earth.

Please join your heart and mind with the hearts and minds of our Father-Mother God, the entire Company of Heaven, and the I Am presence of every man, woman, and child on Earth. As you recite this invocation, know that you are the open door that no one can shut. You are the Light of the world and the time for you to shine is now.

This is an invocation that has been given to us by the Company of Heaven. It is stated in the first person, so that you will experience this activity of Light personally and tangibly, but know that you are simultaneously serving as a surrogate on behalf of every man, woman, and child on Earth.

Know that as you are lifted up, all of life is being lifted up with you. As you invoke the patterns associated with the New Earth for yourself you are also invoking these patterns of perfection on behalf of every person on Earth. With the assistance of each person's I Am presence, this will be accomplished in perfect alignment with every person's Divine plan and the highest good for all concerned. And so we begin…

I Am One with my Omniscient, Omnipresent, Omnipotent Father-Mother God, the cosmic I Am, All That Is.

And I Am One with the entire Company of Heaven.

I invoke the I Am presence of each member of my family, my friends, and the entire family of humanity to take command of this activity of Light, which I now invoke on behalf of myself and every person on Earth. Beloved ones, breathe the patterns of perfection for the New Earth through every person's Heart Flame in perfect alignment with his or her Divine plan and the highest good for all concerned.

I Am the open door for the patterns of perfection for the New Earth.

I Am inbreathing these patterns from the mental and emotional strata of Earth into my Heart Flame, and I am breathing these patterns for the New Earth out through my Heart Flame to bless all life on this planet.

As I breathe these patterns into the physical plane of Earth through my Heart Flame, my Father-Mother God and the entire Company of Heaven expand my efforts a thousand times, a thousand fold.

I now breathe through my Heart Flame and the Heart Flames of all humanity the patterns of the New Earth.

I Am breathing through my Heart Flame into the physical plane of Earth the patterns for the infinite flow of God's abundance, opulence, financial freedom, and the God-supply of all good things. (pause)

I Am breathing through my Heart Flame into the physical plane of Earth the patterns for eternal youth, vibrant health, radiant beauty, and flawless form. (pause)

I Am breathing through my Heart Flame into the physical plane of Earth the patterns for perfect health habits, including eating and drinking habits, exercise, work, relaxation and recreation habits, and spiritual devotion, meditation and contemplation habits. (pause)

I Am breathing through my Heart Flame into the physical plane of Earth the patterns for Divine family life, loving relationships, adoration, Divine Love, Divine sexuality, true understanding, clear and effective communication, open heart sharing, oneness, and the unification of the family of humanity. (pause)

I Am breathing through my Heart Flame into the physical plane of Earth the patterns for eternal peace, harmony, balance, and reverence for ALL life. (pause)

I Am breathing through my Heart Flame into the physical plane of Earth the patterns for self-empowerment, success, fulfillment, Divine purpose, a rewarding career, self-esteem, spiritual development, enlightenment, Divine consciousness, and Divine perception. (pause)

I Am breathing through my Heart Flame into the physical plane of Earth the patterns that will initiate open heart and mind telepathic communication with the Company of Heaven and the angelic and elemental kingdoms. (pause)

I Am breathing through my Heart Flame into the physical plane of Earth the patterns that will inspire creativity through music, singing, sound, toning, dance, movement, art, and education. (pause)

I Am breathing through my Heart Flame into the physical plane of Earth the patterns for laughter, joy, playfulness, fun, elation, enthusiasm, self-expression, bliss, ecstasy, wonder, and awe. (pause)

I Am breathing through my Heart Flame into the physical plane of Earth the patterns that will tangibly manifest Heaven on Earth and a renaissance of Divine Love. (pause)

I now ACCEPT and KNOW through every fiber of my being that these patterns of perfection for the New Earth have been successfully breathed through my Heart Flame into the physical plane.

I also ACCEPT and KNOW that my I Am presence will intensify these patterns every day, with every breath I take, until the New Earth is physically manifest, and this sweet Earth and ALL her Life are wholly ascended and FREE!

In deep humility, Divine Love, and gratitude I decree, it is done. And so it is.

Beloved I Am, Beloved I Am, Beloved I Am.

Within the oneness of all Life there is no such thing as 'us and them.' All Life is interconnected, interdependent, and interrelated. What affects one facet of Life affects all Life. What blesses and enhances one part of Life, blesses and enhances all Life.

~Patricia Cota-Robles

About Patricia Cota-Robles

Patricia is cofounder and president of the nonprofit, educational organization, New Age Study of Humanity's Purpose, which sponsors her work and the Annual World Congress on Illumination.

Patricia was a marriage and family counselor for 20 years. She now spends her time freely sharing the information she is receiving from the Beings of Light in the realms of illumined Truth. She is an internationally known teacher and has taught workshops in many countries. Patricia participated in the First Global Earth Summit held in Rio de Janeiro, Brazil. She also had the honor of being a presenter at the Call to World Peace from the Universal Brotherhood gathering in Istanbul, Turkey, and the Symphony of Peace Prayers, which was a gathering of over ten thousand people that took place at sacred Mt. Fuji in Japan.

For more information, *www.eraofpeace.org*

The Healing
Journey of the Soul

☼

By Richard Waterborn

*Our Soul is on a journey which began eons ago and
which, for most of us, will continue for centuries yet.
Increasing our understanding of that journey and
appreciating who we really are enriches our lives
beyond measure.*

~Dr Brenda Davies

Have you ever had a strong yearning to go home? Not
to your actual house, or your childhood home (though
these places may hold some resonance of this yearning), but to
some rather vaguely defined yet clearly known place where we
feel we truly belong: at peace, at rest, connected, loved, and
accepted unconditionally. Like the salmon which traverses
thousands of miles of ocean to return to the very same river
in which it was spawned, our souls are drawn to return to
their Source. Just as scientists are still trying to discover how
animals such as the salmon or migratory birds can accomplish
such astonishing feats of navigation, the guiding force that
draws and guides the Soul to its destination is shrouded in
mystery. Unlike the enormous distances spanned by a bird's
migratory passage, the Soul's path is an inward one, a journey
without distance, measureable by some less tangible yardstick
than miles or degrees of longitude, guided by a compass so
subtle it almost defies description.

Like attracts like: we are essentially spiritual beings
experiencing life as incarnated human beings, each one of us a
spark of the Divine Light of Source, seemingly separate yet in
reality all part of the One. This spiritual umbilicus can neither

be lost nor severed, however much we may have forgotten or blocked its gentle call to remember who we really are and return. So often I hear clients say wistfully, "I just want to go home." Sadly, the promise of peace and rest of this home is often equated with death and a desire to hasten its inevitable approach. While death does return us to an awareness of our spiritual nature and the huge love and compassion we can access from the disembodied state, final and complete rest and peace, the ultimate homecoming is the goal and result of the healing journey: the decision to become consciously and actively involved in the path of your own Soul through the vast Ocean of Eternity. When this goal is achieved in life, rather than previewed in death, we become enlightened beings, free and at peace.

The Soul: the ka and the ba

We in the west have a rather confused idea about the Soul— if indeed we even recognize that we have one—or perhaps put more accurately that we are a Soul! The ancient Egyptians had a deeply developed knowledge and understanding of the Soul and how to become consciously engaged in its development. They called it the ba, and depicted it as a bird, sometimes bearing a human face to show its spiritual nature. The ascended god Horus is depicted with a falcon's head on a human body, showing that he has attained full God-realization. The ba is closely related to what they called the ka, translated as the essential energy body or etheric template. The ba (Soul) is our individual guide and mentor, mediating between our human form and our spiritual source, like a migratory bird flying back and forth between different continents. It is the Soul which monitors our spiritual development and progress from an objective point of view, detached from the dramas of the incarnate ego. It views our experiences in embodied human form from the perspective of Source. We might think of it as our "God-self."

The ka, on the other hand, is our personal record keeper, recording all the significant events and experiences of an entire lifetime in the etheric body as what are often called 'cellular memories.' It is depicted as a pair of outstretched arms, extended vertically upwards from the elbows. As well as signifying both reverence for and the embracing of life, in full-size statues or carvings, the arm-span describes the dimensions of the actual energy body. In the elaborate Egyptian tombs there is always carved a "false doorway" for the free passage of the ka as it continues its homeward journey after the physical body has died. The family of the deceased bring offerings of food and drink to nourish the ka, knowing that it is a living entity, which like all life-forms requires nourishment. Prayers and incantations are recited to aid and support the ka in its quest to return to the Light of Source. In modern times Kirlian photography has clearly imaged the etheric body, and demonstrated that it continues to exist independently of the physical body. Even when a limb has been lost or amputated, a kirlian photograph shows the limb still attached to, and integrated with the rest of the etheric body. When we see a ghost we are seeing the ka of the deceased, trapped on the Earth plane.

Setting the life course: Soul learning and development

It is the Soul which determines the circumstances and conditions of each incarnation; each venture into the vast school of physical life. It does so in order to maximize the learning potential for the individual spiritual entity depending on its stage of development, to realize (make real) that which exists as potential within. The Soul sets up the optimal situation for our spiritual development; the conditions which afford the greatest opportunity to learn and perfect whatever is most necessary for our progress on the homeward journey. These are not material lessons, but lessons of Love; the same Divine Love from which we have sprung. What are these lessons? Ultimately Love is itself both the lesson and the learner! The "curriculum" includes learning to love and accept our Self—that precious gift with which we are entrusted, developing acceptance of others and compassion for all, learning to both give and receive, and realizing that they are one and the same. The greatest single lesson is that we are all One, connected to the Source of all life and love, and that our thoughts and therefore our actions do not leave their source; that any harmful thoughts we hold about others only serve to separate us from our true nature, whereas kind loving thoughts return us to the awareness of oneness. This is in effect the Law of Karma, that all thoughts, words, and deeds set in motion a ripple effect, which eventually returns to their author, allowing them to experience the effects for themselves. "As you sow, so shall you reap;" "Do unto others as you would have them do to yourself;" "What goes around comes around" are all well-known axioms which express this law. It is pure self-directed learning. There is no one or nothing other than yourself involved.

How do we undertake such a curriculum? As spiritual beings we tend to learn through polarity, or opposition, in a similar way to our human predilection for learning through adversity. Imagine for a moment that, after some intense self-reflection, you realize that you need to develop the quality of courage. What would you do to achieve this? Take yourself off for a pamper weekend at a luxurious spa? Probably not (although for someone with issues of not caring for them self this could indeed be a courageous choice)! Perhaps you might enroll in a fire-walking workshop, or take a course of parachute jumping... some activity in which you are confronted by your fear and required to dig deep within, to contact the latent seed of courage and nurture it into a strong, permanent personal attribute. This is the way we grow and evolve at a spiritual level as well. As the Soul prepares for the next incarnation it gravitates towards the circumstances best suited to the most significant lessons and developing the most important understandings, qualities, and wisdom for the stage or level of evolution appropriate to the individual. Not just parents and family, but social, cultural, and wider parameters are integral to this preparation.

When all is prepared, the stage set, the Ba "calls" to the Ka to connect with the embryo whereupon it begins its physical, psycho-neural-emotional development shaped and directed by the etheric information encoded within the ka. Far from the tabula rasa (blank slate) presumed by material science, the newly incarnated being is, from the very beginning, endowed with a significant legacy that is epigenetic rather than genetic in its origins. The wisdom, skills, talents, and knowledge accrued in previous incarnations may emerge at a young age, and the youthful bearer of such gifts is deemed to be precocious, even perhaps a genius. Likewise, birthmarks, defects, unusual sensitivities, tendencies or idiosyncrasies can often be traced back to outstanding issues from the previous incarnation, carried forward by the ka as important reference points in the ongoing healing and learning experiences, which continue from one lifetime to the next until fully integrated. It is important to point out here that serious birth defects, deformities, or handicaps are not punishments handed out by some judgmental god for misdeeds committed in a previous life.

The veil of forgetting

However, it is at this crucial point of reincarnation that the big problem (or challenge) arises. As we cross the veil between spiritual and physical existence we forget who we are and where we have come from! This amnesia is comparable to what we experience during the 24-hour diurnal cycle, in which we also experience two vastly different realities. While asleep we dream, and the dream-world with all its intense and sometimes exotic experiences, is our only reality. We have no awareness of either the fact that we are dreaming, nor that we were previously "awake." Then when we wake up, we rapidly re-enter the waking reality and forget whatever we dreamed about. The important point to understand is that whilst we are in either state of consciousness—dream-state or awake—it is our one and only reality. It is exactly the same when we "wake up" and find our Self in a physical body in a material world.

So we develop and begin to explore our world, our family, our body, as if for the first time, and encounter and respond to the different situations, relationships, and challenges with absolutely no recognition that we are embarking on a program of spiritual development that was designed for us by our own Soul! This situation, being thrown into life apparently blindfolded from a spiritual point of view, is not a mistake, nor is it deliberately intended to confound us. It is to ensure that the learning is real, that the choices, decisions, actions, reactions, and responses we make and undertake come from our own, God-given, freewill. Only then can we, as spiritual beings, part of the One Source, truly grow and return to full realization of our Divine nature. And only then can the One, Source of all life, grow and explore Itself through us. We are already a part of God-Goddess and share in the creative freedom to explore and enjoy our divinity through freewill. This is both the mystery and the miracle of the homeward journey of the Soul.

Signposts on the homeward journey

We do, however, have an in-built, reliable guide to restore our "spiritual sight" and to once again become consciously aware of our true nature and the journey we are on. Among the cellular memories held and carried forward by the ka are sanskars: a Sanskrit word meaning "scars or grooves of the Soul." The most significant, definitive, and intense experiences of a lifetime leave a deep imprint in the etheric body containing all the associated physical, emotional, and mental traces. During the next incarnation these signals become activated in the subconscious mind rather like an alarm going off repeatedly. Like all such projections of energy this causes us to unconsciously call in and manifest relationships and situations, which are in some way a replay of the original event recorded in the sanskar. Whilst the personnel (the roles) may vary, the essential experience is the same, or will unerringly trigger the same reactions. The unhealed issue, the unlearned lesson, is repeated over and over until we finally heal it, which involves a complete understanding on all levels (see my chapter on Healing the Past in *The Light: A Book of Wisdom*). Once healed, and the lesson has been learned, we are free to move on, to continue our Soul journey, now conscious of our spiritual identity, which became evident through the healing.

My client case notes contain thousands of examples of such sanskars, each one a unique and remarkable "sign-post" for the individual concerned. One particularly poignant story which stands out in memory was of an elderly woman who had come to heal, among other things, a severe anxiety condition. She was a very cultured woman and a highly accomplished pianist. Every time she was about to perform in public she would suffer the most crippling anxiety attacks, so intense that eventually she gave up public recitals. Strangely, when practicing or playing alone, she remained perfectly calm. During the healing session I regressed her to get to the root cause of this peculiar affliction, whereupon the following deeply moving account emerged from her subconscious mind. Her mother, a Jewess, was also an accomplished pianist, prominent on the concert platforms of Europe in the decade before the outbreak of World War Two. Soon after the war began, she, along with millions of her compatriots, was rounded up and consigned to a concentration camp. She was pregnant. Whilst her husband and other members of her family were taken to the gas chambers, her life was spared on account of her notorious talent, and she was compelled to entertain the officers of the camp with frequent recitals. One can easily imagine her anguish at having to obey and give pleasure to the very people who had murdered her loved ones, yet for the sake of her unborn baby, feeling she had no choice but to comply. Every time she was called upon to perform her body was flooded with extremely intense feelings of grief, angst, and hatred for those who were effectively torturing her. Intimately connected both umbilically and energetically, her baby's tiny body shared this emotional holocaust, whilst also hearing the exquisite sounds of her mother's beautiful piano playing. As we now know, and is scientifically proven, intrauterine learning is not just a fact, but an incredibly deep and enduring form of conditioned learning. The woman survived and gave birth to a healthy daughter—my client—who grew up to follow in her mother's footsteps and become a pianist herself. It was only when she embarked on a public career that the buried, dramatic effects of her mother's ordeal became apparent. (I am pleased to relate that after her treatment she was able to perform publicly without the intense emotional reaction.)

The two paths: love and fear

Cellular memory, which has become a popular term for describing our fundamental organismic memory, is something of a misnomer since the remembered information is primarily held by the etheric body in energetic form, in much the same way as a silicon chip holds all the data of a computer or other such device. However, it is this information which does indeed shape and determine our lives at a cellular level. It was the biologist Bruce Lipton (see his chapter, *Creating Heaven on Earth*, on page 220) whose outstanding research work conclusively demonstrated that our cells grow and function not under the direction of the DNA contained in their nuclei, but in fact receive their "instructions" from an external source; the sum total of information recorded and remembered in our ka or energy body channeled through the subconscious mind, which pervades our physical body. Lipton showed that our cells have two essential modes of functioning: growth and expansion, or defense and contraction. Under normal conditions our cells replicate, grow, and carry out their specific tasks in the body in optimal fashion promoting and sustaining healthy development and living. However, when we are under stress, the cells go into defense mode, shutting down their normal activity to divert energy to the essential core body processes. It is when such stress becomes chronic that the prolonged suspension of normal, growth-orientated cellular activity gives rise to problems and eventually to disease.

It is here that we can begin to get some insight into the connection between physical health and the larger picture of the healing journey of the Soul, and understand how we can become a conscious participant in that journey. The primary spiritual lesson we all are called to learn is that of Love. And it is when we are in an emotional / mental state of Love that we are energetically connected to all Life, to the essential oneness of which we are a part, rather than apart from. It has been scientifically proven that when in this state of Love, our cells, organs, indeed our entire physiology, function at their absolute optimal level. Fear is the polar opposite state to Love. It is defined and generated by the perceived experience of being alone (rather than at One), separate from all other beings, from life itself; reliant for survival on the fragile ego. Fear wears many faces: anxiety, anger, jealousy, depression… virtually every negative emotional state we can name is ultimately derived from fear. Whatever its outward guise, fear automatically generates stress and tension in the body, which leads to cellular shut-down. And when this becomes a chronic condition, as it is for so many of us in today's world, this inevitably causes some form of imbalance, dysfunction, and ultimately disease. Oftentimes it is only when we receive some "sledge-hammer guidance" in the form of a serious health problem that we begin to heed the call and embark on our own healing journey.

The body, with the exquisite sensitivities of its organs, tissues, cells, and sophisticated nervous system, is our primary communication instrument. Every cell and tissue is permeated by the multi-layered energy body with its archive of memories and information. It is the physical location of what we term the subconscious mind—that vast transpersonal repository of experiential information and self-knowledge. Every biological function, right down to the division and replication of our cells, is entrained by the emotional and mental signals emanating from the energy body; every circadian biorhythm resonating to its frequencies. It is by tuning in and listening intently to our bodies and feelings that we can really know what is going on inside us. Indeed, I have come to believe that this is the primary reason for having a body! The mind, powerful though it is, can block, rationalize or deny the information it receives from the body. We can live in our heads, apparently safe and immune to life's challenges whilst imbalances and disturbances at an emotional level are ignored, until we wake up one day to discover we have a serious problem. It is my clinical experience that a great many people are actually living "out of their body," that is to say with their energy body and awareness withdrawn from the lower body.

Compassion: the way home

How do we begin to cultivate such a communication? If Love is the ultimate lesson, then compassion is the means by which we learn it. We have learned to think of compassion as something we should have for others, however, like all such qualities, it has to begin with our Self. Whether we are looking within or out into the "real world," compassion is the practice through which we unerringly connect to the underlying reality of our Soul and speed our healing journey home. Literally "being with passion" compassion is more a practice than a quality, although we become more compassionate through the practice. Sometimes defined as feeling without thought, compassion enables us to connect directly to the energetic life-stream within our body, which is passion, and the organismic knowing and wisdom to which it gives access. This profound level of awareness, reaching far deeper than our intellectual or cognitive knowing, is a faculty we share with all life forms: animals, plants, even minute unicellular organisms, through which we connect directly to what science now calls the Intelligent Life Field, the fundamental creative consciousness of Source itself. In order to do so we first need to relinquish all claims or attempts to judge our Self, another person, or Life itself. In fact, we quickly realize through the practice of compassion that all judgments are nothing more than our own projections. Instead, we use the faculty of discernment, a simple innate knowing whether something, or someone, is intrinsically beneficial, life enhancing or affirming of us, personally, or if it is intrinsically harmful, diminishing or self-negating. We are not called upon to judge whether something or someone is good or bad, right or wrong, only to take responsibility for our Self and its needs, discerning what is good for us.

We are not alone on the journey! Through compassion we realize that the world, everything in it, our selves, others, and our relationships are all part of our journey home, reflecting facets of our Self which have been lost, forgotten, denied, or suppressed, offering us endless opportunities to truly know our Self, to learn, to heal, to grow. Instead of judging, blaming, criticizing, or disapproving of others, compassion invites us to look instead into the mirror they represent, reflecting and illuminating the obscurity of our own shadow, inviting us to go within, heal our deepest wounds, and retrieve the lost or forgotten fragments of our Divine wholeness. There is a more personal and intimate group of relationships known as our Soul family; kindred souls in whose company we are making this journey, tracking together the undulating path from one incarnation to another. Often these souls "show up" as family or other close and significant relationships, although not always in the same position. Roles, relationships, even gender are interchangeable in this powerful learning academy. Often we, as Soul consciousness, need to explore and experience all possible sides, polarities, and extremes of human experience in order to come into balance with it and integrate the lesson in a complete and whole way. Parent-child, brother-sister, lover-beloved, victim-perpetrator, abuser-abused. Through stepping into these and myriad other roles from all possible sides and perspectives we acquire the empowering wisdom and understanding that comes from directly experiencing the consequences of our own thoughts, intentions, and actions.

In this co-creative, self-directed learning situation, the

true practice of compassion accepts each Soul's experience unconditionally, and honors the sacredness of both the learner and the lesson. Once we recognize that our experience mirrors and reveals our Divine mission to know our Self in all possible ways, then clearly it is impossible to judge one's Self, a life event, or the actions and choices of another, as right or wrong, good or bad, but rather as a perfect expression of our quest to know the One. Anything that is not an expression of love is a cry for love or a search for love. Instead of the apparent flaws, defects, and misdeeds we perceive in others we can hear and respond to the vicious judgments we have passed on our Selves and behold the harsh self-imposed punishments under which we labor and suffer. When we see the Truth revealed in the Light and understanding of compassion then we are finally free to claim the ultimate gift of healing: forgiveness. Forgiveness of the world, of others, but most crucially forgiveness of our Self. This is the final release from the suffering, the delusional torment of our perceived separation from our Source, the blessed moment when we reawaken to the consciousness of who we really are, our Divine nature.

Awakening from the dream

In my profession as a healer I have been privileged to facilitate and witness this sacred moment of awakening and realization countless times. Whilst profound insights can occur at any time, it is usually during the clearing and lifting of the sanskars, the "Soul imprints," that the most complete and powerful realization dawns. The experiences which cause these memories to be so deeply etched into the ka or energy body are usually extremely intense, involving pain and suffering at both a physical and emotional level, often to the point of death or near-death, at which moment the ka detaches itself from the physical body. Under regression we follow the journey of the ka back to the Light from where the traumatic experience can be safely reviewed, understood, and integrated on all levels: physical, emotional, mental, and spiritual. As this integration progresses and the sanskar is cleared, the Light body can once again fully reconnect with the physical body, an exquisite sensation of deep peace and oneness. Simultaneously, the mind opens to the profound presence of the Soul, our spiritual nature, and the inner senses behold the awesome vista of the Soul's journey homeward.

Such moments of awakening can happen in many other situations, such as near-death experiences, out-of-body experiences, spontaneous moments of heightened awareness, mystical experiences, and so on. Whatever the event or its cause, the central realization of Soul consciousness is the same. These moments, however brief, are life-changing and redefine the basis from which we live. Once we have awakened to the Truth that we are souls, spiritual beings on our way back home to our Source, then we consciously participate in this journey and the desire to know and understand our Self more and more deeply becomes the guiding Light and force in our life. As we seek, we find. When we sincerely ask, then guidance and direction are given, signs and pointers appear to direct us to the next learning experience or relationship. The more we are willing to see everything we encounter, everything and everyone who crosses our path as a mirror, as a teacher, as an opportunity to learn, heal and grow, the more rapidly we progress along the homeward path. Eventually we reach that moment of enlightenment when we realize that we are already home, and that we had never really left, where, in the immortal words of TS Eliot, we "return to the place from which we started, and know it for the first time."

*Like the Atlantic salmon traversing thousands of miles
of ocean to return to the same river in which it was
spawned, our souls are inexorably drawn to return to
their Source.*

~**Richard Waterborn**

About Richard Waterborn

Richard Waterborn developed an early interest in healing due to the near death of his mother who sought help from many of the healers of the time.

In his twenties he moved to Ireland where an intense journey of personal healing and transformation began, leading to profound spiritual experiences and a life changing connection to the Ascended Master, Hedekhan Babaji.

In 1994, he met and studied with Drunvalo Melchizedec and became a certified facilitator of the Flower of Life. Since, he has combined a busy healing practice, teaching metaphysical and spiritual wisdom and leading sacred journeys of remembering to locations such as Egypt, Peru, Mexico, and the ancient sites of Ireland and England.

Richard divides his healing and teaching work between Ireland and Spain.

For more information, *www.richardwaterborn.com*

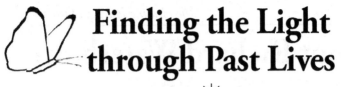

Finding the Light through Past Lives

☼

By Melanie Hoffmann

Life is a tragedy when seen in close-up, but a comedy in long-shot.

~Charlie Chaplin

It is said that one must believe it to see it. But for me, it happened in reverse. I saw and yet I didn't want to believe, until eventually the evidence became so strong that I had no other choice but to accept there was more to life than what I perceived as my reality. I was brought up in a very conservative environment where the most attention a subject such as reincarnation would receive was a raised eyebrow. As a result I felt extremely confused when I accidentally travelled into past lives. I did not purely see pictures that can easily be construed as tricks played by the mind. Instead, I relived parts of previous lifetimes that delivered my greatest fears to me on a silver platter; fears that I had abandoned into the dungeon of my Soul.

Learning about past lives is a painful yet liberating experience. It's not the pleasant and beautiful parts that we recall. It's our darkest moments and most fearful memories. And if we are courageous enough to take an honest look at these, we will eventually discover the greatest treasure there is. Because underneath the many layers of fears, we will discover our own Light.

What are past lives?

Past lives are the several incarnations on Earth that a Soul has travelled through in the vehicle of a body, previous to the current incarnation. Like changing trains and planes on a trip around the world, each incarnation or lifetime is experienced in a new body; a shell that we humans identify with. Like everything in the Universe, what was once created will one day be destroyed again, as will our bodies that were created out of semen and an egg cell. Upon its death, the body will rot and return to Mother Earth. All that remains is the Soul, our true core. For the Soul, death is purely a transition. It will live on; formless, infinite, and eternal. And at certain intervals, it will return to Earth again within a new body and behind a new mask.

The many different bodies we use for our several incarnations project an incorrect image to us. We see different bodies belonging to different lifetimes, so we believe those incarnations to be separate from each other. But they are not. They all belong to the same stream, flowing without cease. The passenger is still the same passenger as the one who was present one thousand years ago. And the luggage has been collected since the very first day of the very first incarnation. We all carry a suitcase of fears that we are here to experience and unpack. Fear has many faces, such as doubt, pride, anger, greed, jealousy, and so on. Those fears have been collected over our many incarnations. Down here on Earth, we mostly believe that our fears are tied to possible future scenarios. But our greatest fears spring from our subconscious memory, which remembers tragedies, big and small, from past lives. Nothing in our current lifetime exists by coincidence. No fear, no desire, no interest, no habit. By fearing something to occur, what we're really doing is remembering that this very scenario has occurred before, so what we truly fear is that it may repeat itself. Without a certain situation having occurred to us before, the fear would not exist within us.

Let me give you a simple example. A few summers ago, Philine, my Chihuahua, was stung by a bee. Within minutes, her little paw had swollen to three times its size. The pain she was in was almost unbearable for me to watch. And still today, whenever Philine sees or hears a bee, she immediately runs inside the house to hide. Before the incident, a bee was just a bee to her; an innocent, tiny insect, happily buzzing through the summer sky. But since that day, she associates the painful bee-sting with a bee every time she sees one, and what remains is an unpleasant memory that sets off her alarm bells within seconds.

The majority of our fears are nothing but alarm bells going off, as a result of subconsciously remembering past life events. Consider why a person fears dogs without ever having had a bad experience with one in this lifetime. Or why does someone fear crossing a bridge without recalling a particular accident while doing so? Or someone might be extremely greedy. Although he runs a very successful business his subconscious remembers losing his entire wealth. The Truth is that our subconscious remembers it all. The energies of past events are all trapped in our system. I, for instance, am absolutely terrified of snakes. Or better said, I am terrified of the consequence of such an encounter. From traveling into my past lives, I now know that I was once bitten by a snake, which caused my sudden death. And although I'm aware of what causes my fear, I still cannot let go of it. It's a fear that almost paralyzes me, and I'm pretty certain that it's a fear I won't overcome in this lifetime. And I don't have to. The beauty of life is that we have freewill. We decide what lessons we will conquer and we alone set the pace. There is no hurry in life other than our own impatience.

What we really discover in past lives

We have come here to evolve and to reawaken to love. I do not particularly like the term 'learn' as I don't see life as a classroom but rather as a playground where we come to play until we remember who we truly are. And by remembering who we are, I do not mean remembering the identity we took on in our previous lifetimes. This identity, together with the circumstances that surround us, are just the trigger to our fears that we are here to let go of. We will eventually remember who we truly are by discovering who we are *not*. What we are is very simple. The innermost core of every being is love, which is Light in its purest form. No matter what our past looks like, how much good or bad we have done, our core exists of nothing but love. The core of a sinner does not differentiate itself from the core of a saint. Our core is pure Light. But what differs from individual to individual are the many layers of fear wrapped around its core that prevents it from shining bright. Those layers are like shutters that imprison the Light within us and throw a dark shadow onto our being. By remembering who we are, we remember the love—the Light—within us and we stop identifying ourselves with the layers of darkness, finally able to let go of them. So it's not about letting the Light in, but about letting the Light out.

From traveling into past lives, I learned that my shell, the many different identities I had taken on in several past lives, is the least important factor. I know this is what we are usually most curious about, as we grant our identity such importance. We want to know who we were. Were we a man or a woman? Were we rich or poor? Where did we live? What was our profession? Who were we in love with? And so on. The Truth is, you might have been a famous actor, winning an Oscar for some spectacular performance, yet you will never find out about it in past life visions. Why is that? Because, in most cases, it doesn't matter. When this actor left his lifetime behind, he didn't take the Oscar with him. He will have taken the memory of it with him, and in his next lifetime he might find that he loves watching the Oscars on television or he might feel drawn towards recognition in form of a diploma or a trophy, but the true weight in his suitcase once he travels on are the fears he needs to let go of. And those are the exact fears that you will relive when traveling into past lives. You will discover the same fears, tied to fresh scenarios in your current life that purely serve to pull the trigger. Eventually, through awakening to this game of life, you will begin to see that we all take it far too seriously.

Having visited several past lives, I found that a pattern

begins to reveal itself and a fine, red thread connects not just the lives of one Soul alone, but the lives of entire Soul families. Our lives are all interwoven. And suddenly, everything seems clear and simple. What we eventually learn is that our fears are no more than collected souvenirs that have built a tower around our core over several incarnations. But our core is untouchable. It shines bright at all times. It is purely our fears that prevent our Light from illuminating our path.

An imperfect perfection

Before our Soul decides to reincarnate again, its upcoming journey is carefully prepared together with our Soul families and guides on what is commonly known as the other side. It's not much different from making travel arrangements. Depending on our luggage—aka our fears, desires, interests, and so on—we choose all kinds of possible scenarios to occur and familiar souls to reunite with along our journey. Those scenarios and souls are chosen according to the fears we are eager to strip ourselves of and the purpose we are here to fulfill. Once we truly understand this, we begin to see the perfection in every imperfection, and the Divine in the greatest chaos. Because that is when we realize that every situation has a hidden lesson, and that every person we meet along our journey is a teacher in disguise. Nothing here on Earth happens to us. We have made the arrangements for it all well in advance. How we now handle it is entirely our choice. It is up to us to step out of the victim-stance, take responsibility for our life, and choose love over fear.

From traveling into past lives, I learned how our situation keeps repeating itself over and over again. The Truth is that our situation won't change unless we change. And positive change is the result of growth, which is exactly what we are here for. Our many lifetimes are not that different from each other. On the outside, they seem worlds apart, but on the inside, the same old story keeps repeating itself, like a broken vinyl record that gets stuck in the same place every time you play it. It amazes me how we don't get worn out by our own issues. But no, patiently we continue playing this game called life, knowing deep down within that eventually we will rise above our issues and fears to shine our most beautiful Light.

I know this is easier said than done. Life here on Earth can appear tough and it can actually be tough when we are cut off from the bigger picture of life and caught in this tiny box, which we mistake for our reality.

The greatest and most valuable Truth I've learned from traveling into past lives is that 'everything is and everything is not.' This Truth applies to just about everything in life. It all depends on where we are viewing things from. Take death, for example. Portraying the bigger picture of life, death is an illusion. Death is no more than a transition, like our birth. No matter how often we come and go, we keep on existing. But when portraying the smaller picture of life from down here on Earth, death is real. We enter this world in a physical body and some day we leave again. We disappear and are no longer here. The body and person we cast off one day will never return in the same form. What will return is our core, but not the identity we have taken on in this lifetime. So yes, death is an illusion. And yes, death is real. Both versions are fact. Both versions are true. Everything is and everything is not.

No matter how terrible this smaller picture of ours may temporarily appear, seen from above and within the bigger picture of life, all is fine. There is nothing to fear, ever. And no matter how hopeless or senseless things seem, there is a place where everything makes sense. There is an answer to every question and a 'because' to every why. But the 'because' often belongs to the bigger picture and is hard for us to grasp here on Earth. Our fears are bound to the smaller picture. In the bigger picture, only love exists. The bigger picture is a place of Truth where illusion finds no fertile ground. Illusion does not mean that something isn't real. It means that we perceive something for what it is not, as we are portraying it from a different angle.

Yogi Bhajan said, "If you can't see God in all, you can't see

God at all." Seeing the Divine in everything is exactly what happens to us when traveling into past lives, and with it we begin to awaken to the greater Truth of life.

soul mates and life lessons

What matters and what we are here for is our spiritual unfoldment. Everything that occurs in our lives, no matter how insignificant it appears, has meaning and is there for our spiritual development. It is said that once the pupil is ready, the master will appear. Many of us wait in anticipation for that moment to arrive, but that moment is already here. The master is by our side, always. It is our mother, our father, our siblings, our friends, our enemies, our pets, our neighbors, the waiter at our favorite restaurant, the newspaper salesman, and the random stranger that passes us daily. Only when we are ready to accept everyone as our teacher, are we ready to grow spiritually.

The many people we meet along our journey are mostly souls we have spent countless lifetimes with before. We have large Soul families that keep reuniting in different constellations. I compare it to a theatrical play in which the roles change according to who might play a certain part best this time around. That means that your lover in this lifetime might have been your father or brother in a previous lifetime. Your yoga teacher might have been your best friend, and your sister might have been a work colleague. No matter what the constellation is in this very moment, trust that it is perfect. Every person in our lives plays the perfect role, no matter how imperfect, misplaced, or disturbing it may seem.

Often, the people who hurt us the most are the souls closest to us. They are the souls that take on the unpopular roles in order to help us grow. The problem is that we do not remember the arrangements we made with these souls before our current incarnation. Whenever we have an encounter with a person we don't like, or whenever we face a situation that we do not feel at ease with, it has to do with our own inner issues that we are here to overcome. Never with the outer situation or encounter. Only with ourselves.

So who are our soul mates? We all want to believe there is one person out there, meant only for us. Our other half. The one person who makes us whole. However, the one and only person that can make us whole, is our Self. As long as we haven't found the love within, we are not going to find it without. But what we will find in every relationship, is the perfect match. Not the kind of match that will reflect our wishes and dreams, but the kind of match that will reflect our deepest fears. Our soul mates are not the ones we had in mind as the perfect fit. True soul mates are the ones that tear our walls down, make us bleed and fall apart. They are the ones that rip old wounds open from many lifetimes ago, and give us the chance to finally heal.

From my own experience, I know that the more intimate a love relationship has been in this lifetime, the more baggage—or karma—we had brought along from the past as a couple. There has not been one single boyfriend with whom life has been rosy. It is actually the contrary. Often, we have faced extremely difficult relationships in our past lives—and I'm not only talking about love relationships—where we would have best been described as fierce enemies. Even murder happened. Having visions of past lives and seeing where we came from, was initially shocking and disturbing for me. But today, I see the beauty in it. And it all comes down to love. We have come here to find love in every imaginable facet; to discover the love within ourselves and to be love. And what teaches us a greater lesson and is more romantic than learning to love our worst enemy?

How to become more aware of past lives

Traces of our past lives are everywhere. Just pay a little attention to your fears, your passions, your interests, and your habits. As a little girl, I loved barbecues. I remember how it drove my father insane when I tried sending smoke signs to my best friend, who lived only a few meters away. Nevertheless, what appeared to be a childish game was a subconscious memory from a lifetime as a Native American. It also worried my mother every time she caught me eating grass in our garden. For me, picking food from Mother Earth was the most natural thing in the world.

Simply pay attention to your everyday habits. Ask yourself questions such as: *which parts of the world do I dream of visiting? Is there a certain culture I feel naturally drawn to? What are my special talents? What comes easily to me? Do I know how to perform a certain task without ever having studied it? What am I passionate about? Is there a specific era I am particularly interested in? Is there a historic movie I love watching? A certain author whose books I love reading? If so, what does he or she write about? What nicknames do my friends give me? Have I ever meet someone feeling like I have known this person for my entire life? Have I ever visited a place, feeling like I have been there before?* The fun facts of our past lives, as I like calling them, lie right before our feet. Most of them are way too obvious.

Light Practice:

A simple and fun thing to do is to start a journal in which you document your wildest dreams, your dullest habits, your greatest interests, and your deepest fears. Split this journal into the aforementioned four sections. This is your journal alone. Nobody else must ever look at it, so be brutally honest. And give yourself time. You mustn't fill the blank pages in one go. Have fun with it and be creative. You may even like to make a small collage of each section; sort of like a small vision board, using pictures from magazines. After a while, you might detect a pattern or a bigger picture will begin to reveal itself. But know that one single wish or fear can spring from several incarnations, as we are a compilation of our entire past. One of my grandest desires, for example, was to adopt a little girl from Nepal. The roots to this desire lay in three different lifetimes.

If it is your true desire to find out about your past lives then do not forget the most important thing: ask. Send your desire out into the Universe and ask for answers. We are constantly surrounded by our guides, who are not allowed to interfere in our life if we don't specifically ask them to. So simply ask. And should the answer be in alignment with your Soul's path, it will be given to you.

Our deepest fears are the hardest to find as they are protected by the ego. But if we are brave enough to take an honest look at our life and the repeating situations we find ourselves in, accepting that we are not the victim, we will discover and master those too. Life is a reflection of our inner state. The more Truth we allow into our lives, the clearer and brighter the reflection becomes.

There is, of course, no secret recipe or magic spell for remembering past lives. But there is one piece of advice I want to give you anyhow: Don't think but *feel*. We are all vibrating energy. And everything in our world and within the entire Universe exists on different frequencies. In order to tune into a higher frequency, we have to raise our vibration. Because only when we match a certain frequency can we experience its reality, meaning that our current reality always depends on our current frequency. Raising our vibration sounds like far more work than it truly is. Go out into nature. Not once in a while, but frequently. Make it your sacred ritual. If you have time to go to the gym, you have time for nature. Get up an hour earlier if needed. That is exactly what I do. And then, feel the nature. Switch off your mind and be present. When I walk with my dog in the mountains, I let her lead the way as her senses are much finer than mine, and she guides me to the most breathtaking places. While we walk, I touch the trees and let the high grass run through my fingers. I stop and smell the flowers. I feel the wind in my hair and the rain on my face. I pick up stones and play with them in my hands. I love how they leave traces of earth in my palm. I treasure my meditations, but the most precious moments for me are those spent free of thought in nature. It's my temple that I visit daily. And although I usually have dirty hands and messy hair when I return home, on a much deeper level, my mind, body, and Soul have been cleansed.

When we truly feel, there is no space left for thought. When we truly feel, we are in the moment. And when we are in the now, time disappears and everything becomes accessible. In reality there is no past or future. Time as we perceive it is an illusion. Everything happens at once, in parallel layers. I am not a scientist, so I can only touch on this Truth. But what I can say is that I have experienced those parallel layers when momentarily caught in two lifetimes at once. When we are in the Now, we escape the illusion of time and we are connected with the entire Universe; with All There Is.

I must admit that I already had psychic abilities as a child without being aware of them. But what fueled my past life travels and deepened my spiritual experiences was a combination of three simple events. Firstly, my dog entered my life. I had not been looking for a pet, but followed my heart when a puppy with water on its lungs needed a loving parent. Secondly, I found myself living in the mountains, in a place where I didn't want to be, but I had no other choice at the time. What I perceived to be a curse transpired to be one of my greatest blessings ever as, together with my dog, I began to explore the natural habitat. Thirdly, a couple of years later, a friend insisted that I join her for yoga, saying that it might cure an injury of mine. In a nutshell, spending lots of time in nature, practicing yoga, meditating, and chanting mantras, changed my life. Today, my dog is my guru, nature is my temple, and yoga is my sacred practice.

Light Practice:

Being psychic is not a special gift but our nature. It is our sixth sense that we block with uncontrolled thoughts and an overfed lifestyle. I compare it to a tube that is momentarily clogged. The best way to clean that tube is to spend regular time in nature and in silence. Busyness has become a fashion that is cutting us off from our core. To connect with nature and to find a moment of silence, I recommend finding a tree to visit daily. Don't switch from tree to tree. Find one specific tree that you feel comfortable with. This doesn't have to be an ancient tree. The tree next to the bus stop or in the local park will do. Give your tree a hug, or if you don't want to be as obvious, lean against it. Start a friendship with it. What might feel awkward at first will turn into the most natural thing in life. Trees are amazing companions. They don't only provide us with oxygen but with the purest of all energies. Put your flat palm against the tree as that will charge your natural batteries and lighten your entire being. Soon you will find further rituals to add to your day. I, for example, talk to the moon and the stars every night when taking my dog for one last walk right before bedtime. Find daily rituals that suit you and then truly commit to them.

Conclusion

Our current lifetime is a sacred gift and yet another opportunity to shift into higher awareness. We are bigger than this life on Earth. Our existence didn't start here and neither will it end here. This is only a small part of a very long journey. We've been here dozens of times before, and we will likely return, so let us be grateful for our time here and experience it to the fullest. We have come here for a purpose. We were not sent here against our will. This was our choice and our choice alone, so may we make the most of it.

> *"We are no more than travelers, who must learn to travel light."*
> ~Melanie Hoffmann

About Melanie Hoffmann

Born and raised in Cologne, Germany, Melanie studied classical ballet according to the syllabus of the Royal Academy of Dance, London, passing her Intermediate examination with Honors. At the age of sixteen, she became a merit scholarship student at the Gus Giordano Dance Center, Chicago, where she was educated in American jazz-dance. For over ten years, she has been passing on her knowledge by teaching young dance students in the United Kingdom, Germany, and Spain.

An injury forced Melanie to give up her dancing career and led her into a yoga studio for the very first time. Not only did yoga soothe her physical pains, but it also released all the blockages in her body. Totally unprepared, she was suddenly connected with the spirit world and travelled into past lives. After recovering from the initial shock, she followed a friend's advice and documented her journey in a personal diary, which resulted in her upcoming book, *Stripped to my Soul.*

Melanie is delighted to be featured in *Experiences from the Light: Ordinary People's Extraordinary Experiences of Transformation, Miracles, and Spiritual Awakening,* compiled and edited by Keidi Keating. She is also a blogger for The Huffington Post.

Currently, Melanie resides in the mountains of Southern Spain. When she is not busy writing, she spends time in nature, together with her furry Soul mate, a Chihuahua named Philine.

For more information, *www.melanie-hoffmann.com*

Peace: For Ourselves and For the World

By Pujya Swamiji

Peace comes from within. Do not seek it without.
~Buddha

Each year, our scientific, technological, medical, and mechanical prowess increases.

Each year, our newfound skills and feats dwarf the achievements of years passed.

Each year, we break through yet another layer of the glass ceiling, accomplishing tasks previously deemed impossible.

Yet, simultaneously and perhaps not coincidentally, each year the number of people killed, maimed, and terrorized by violence in the name of religion also increases. Each year, the number of children orphaned needlessly and senselessly by crimes of hate, terror, and revenge scales new heights.

We pat ourselves on the back as smallpox and polio are eradicated, sparing the lives of innumerable children. Yet, the streets of countless cities worldwide teem with wandering, starving, begging orphans whose parents were killed in the name of God.

Each year, people continue to grow in success financially, buying the newest models of houses, cars, and other material items. Yet, anxiety and stress increase alongside these things, and people are unable to find peace.

Peace—in our world, in our communities, in our families, and within ourselves—has become the greatest need, a common catchphrase, and yet the scarcest commodity.

Without peace—both inner and outer—all else is meaningless. We can spend millions of dollars building posh downtown centers in our cities, but if we are at war with another country, they will bomb those centers to ashes in a second. We can work hard and successfully at our jobs, but if we come home to turmoil in the home, there is no joy in the success obtained at work, for there is no one with whom to share it. We can devote ourselves to obtaining a top education, the highest credentials, and a beautiful figure. However, if we are miserable inside, no outer achievement will ever pacify us.

As rungs on the ladder of eternal harmony, the aspects have to be taken in that sequential order. Even if our ultimate goal is only world peace, still we must start with ourselves. If we are not at peace personally, the best we can hope to achieve for the world is the same temporary, fleeting facade of peace that we have achieved for ourselves. As Mahatma Gandhi so eloquently put it: "We must be the change we want to see in the world."

Inner peace

When you are in peace, you exude peace, manifest peace, and spread peace. When you are in pieces, you exude pieces, manifest pieces, and spread pieces. Ironically it seems that day by day, we become less and less peaceful internally while we are yearning more and more to be calm and centered. Our tempers have become shorter. We have to take pills to alleviate our anxiety and to help us sleep at night. Yet, each day we are striving, searching, and hungering for inner peace.

Peace is, however, not something for which we have to search. Peace is our basic, most fundamental nature. We feel restless, anxious, distressed, and agitated due to the covering of our golden peace with the dirt of various emotions, characteristics, and habits.

There is a beautiful story of a temple in Thailand where for years people worshipped what they thought was a clay statue of the Buddha. One day, by mere chance, one of the workers who was cleaning the statue discovered that beneath inches of tightly-packed clay, the statue was actually solid gold.

Centuries before, to protect it from looters and invaders, the Buddhists had covered the Golden Buddha with clay. None of those who knew its true form survived the invasion and onslaught. Hence, all worshippers thereafter assumed the image was one of clay, until the day, hundreds of years later, the pure gold core was discovered.

The same is true with our own lives. We are golden. We are Divine. We are pure and holy. We are the embodiment of peace itself, at our core. However, that golden core has been covered by layer upon layer of greed, ego, attachment, anger, jealousy, illusion, and desire such that we have come to believe that we are made of these emotions. We have forgotten our true nature.

When we get in touch with our internal divinity, we not only tap into the infinite well of peace within us, but we also become instruments of peace for the world.

"I want peace"

The mantra of today seems to be "I want peace." Every day people tell me this. They all say, "Swamiji. I want peace. Tell me how to find it."

The obstacle and the solution are buried in the statement. What do we have in that statement? An "I," a "want," and a "peace." If we remove the "I" and the "want," what is left? "Peace." We do not have to look for peace, find peace, or create peace. All we have to do is remove the "I" and remove the "want," and peace stands there, in its full glory, as Divine nectar for all the world to imbibe. It is the "I" and the "want" which obscure this treasure from our view and prevent us from reveling in the Truth of our own peaceful natures.

"I"

First let's talk about "I." I is one of the greatest obstacles to peace. I is our ego. I is our sense of ownership, doership, and pride. This I says, "I want to be in the center." We always want to be the ones getting the glory, the appreciation, and the prestige. Even when we don't do anything, still we want to be appreciated. This is our downfall.

So what to do? Surrender. Become humble. Realize everything is due only to God.

In India, in or near every village there is a temple. I remember when I was young, first thing in the morning everyone would go to the temple. Then, in the evenings, on the way home from work, everyone would once again stop at the temple.

This tradition still occurs in almost every village, especially the small ones, every day. People in these small villages have very little in terms of material possessions or comforts. Most of them live below western standards of poverty. Yet, because they have God in the center of their lives, they are in peace.

There is a beautiful mantra, which is perfect for eliminating the ego and surrendering to God. The mantra says:

> *Kaayena vaachaa manasendriyairvaa*
> *Buddhyaatmanaavaa praktriteh svabhaavaat*
> *Karomi yadyat sakalam parasmai*
> *Naaraayanaayeti samarpayaami*

This means, "Oh Lord, whatever I have done, whatever actions I have performed through my speech, through my mind (anything I've thought), through my intellect (anything I've planned, achieved or understood), through my hands or body or through any of my senses—therefore anything at all that I have performed, perceived or thought—it is all due to Your Divine grace and I lay it all humbly at Your holy feet."

When we truly surrender our lives, our actions, and our work to Him, our little individual "I" becomes merged in the big "I," the Universal "I," the Divine "I." Our lives become like drops of water that merge into the Divine Ocean. The tension, stress, arrogance, and separateness melt instantaneously and we become bathed by the great Ocean of Peace.

"Want"

"Want" symbolizes our needs, our desires, and our cravings—our insatiable appetite for more and more. All the advertisements, magazines, movies, TV shows—the entire culture—is aiming to convince us that the deepest joy, the most meaningful experiences, the surest peace can be found in owning the right car, wearing the right brand of jeans, living in the right type of home in the right area of town, or by vacationing in the right resort.

The insidiousness of this indoctrination is that not only is it false, but it is also contradictory. Not only will possessions not provide peace and joy, but the constant struggle for more and more will actually lead us further and further down the road to anxiety, restlessness, anger, and frustration.

If we are looking for deep and lasting joy, if we are yearning to be truly peaceful, we must tear off the veil of Maya and realize that possessions, pleasures, and comfort are not the answer.

I always say, "Expectation is the mother of frustration and acceptance is the mother of peace and joy." If we live without expectations, we will always be in peace. We must accept everything that comes in life as God's Prasad (Divine gift and blessing). Our successes, our failures, our gains, our losses—we must see them all as God's Divine gift to us.

There is a beautiful prayer we chant each morning in our prayers at Parmarth Niketan, which says that we should expect nothing, want nothing, crave nothing other than God. Whatever God gives us and wherever God puts us we should be joyful and grateful, and we should accept it as His Divine gift. As long as our hopes are pinned on material and sensual pleasures and achievements, we will be forever miserable. Only by attaching ourselves to God and God alone will we be able to attain the true Divine state of bliss and joy.

How to become selfless? How to learn to give more? To surrender? Prayer. Peace comes through prayer. It doesn't matter what name you use for God or what language you pray in. You can pray to Lord Krishna in Sanskrit, you can pray to Allah in Arabic, you can pray to Jesus in English, you can pray to Adonai in Hebrew, you can pray to Buddha in Japanese, or you can pray to any other form of the Divine in any other language—it doesn't matter. What matters is that the prayer is earnest, pure, and heartfelt.

Everything is for God. We must offer every thought, every action, and every breath at His holy feet. We must give more and want less. Then, we will know true joy and peace.

Forgiveness

One of the greatest abilities given to human beings, and one of the most important on the spiritual path, is the ability to forgive.

Forgiveness is not condoning someone else's hurtful behavior. Forgiveness is not saying that no mistakes were made. Forgiveness is not inviting the pain or abuse again. Forgiveness does not mean that the perpetrator should not be punished.

Forgiveness means that we, as human beings looking for peace, must release the pain, anger and grudges, which act like a vice on our heart, squeezing our vital energy and life force, suffocating us in their grip. Forgiveness removes the vice from our hearts and allows us to breathe, live, and love freely.

When someone hurts us—knowingly or unknowingly, purposely or accidentally—we have three ways of dealing with that hurt: expression, suppression, or forgiveness. However, the first two options—expression and suppression—really only hurt ourselves, enslaving us to our own emotions. The only option truly is to forgive.

Many people misunderstand forgiveness to be a pardoning or exoneration of the act committed. It is not. Every wrong act and every evil deed will be punished by the Law of Karma. No one is free from the Law of Karma.

Forgiveness is more for ourselves than for the person who

committed the act. Forgiveness means that we are able to separate the person who committed the act from the act itself. It means that the act may be deplorable but the person is still human and therefore has strengths as well as weaknesses, good points as well as negative points. Forgiveness means that we are able to tap into the well of compassion which flows in our hearts and offer some of it to those who have wronged us.

Forgiveness means that we need to move forward, that we do not want to freeze in the moment of pain. When we hold onto our anger it immobilizes us, stopping us from blossoming into the people we are supposed to become and achieving that which we are supposed to achieve.

We hold onto our pain because it identifies who we are. It gives us an excuse for behaving the way we do. It has become such a familiar feeling that, regardless of its self-destructive nature, we cannot let it go. Yet, let it go we must if we want to move forward.

It is not an easy task, but it is an essential task if we want to have any peace in our lives, especially if we want to help spread peace to others.

Let us fill our cup from that infinite ocean of compassion and forgiveness so that we too can step freely, peacefully, and joyfully into the future, leaving the shackles of the past behind. Let us fulfill our unique purpose, our Divine mission here on Earth, rising to our greatest potential—academically, professionally, emotionally, and spiritually. Then we will truly be able to serve as warriors for peace in every situation we encounter.

Peace in the world

Today, our world stands on the brink of destruction. Whether we die from a gunshot wound, from thirst in a drought, from lung cancer due to air pollution, from food poisoning, from a tsunami or hurricane, or from a grenade filled with nails, the end result is the same: untimely death due to preventable, self-induced causes. The human race is on a path of self-destruction, which if not curtailed, will inevitably lead not only to the annihilation of our race but to the dissolution of life as we know it on Earth.

When we talk about peace in the global, international arena, frequently we are simply referring to the cessation of violence. To bring "Peace in the Middle East" means that Israelis and Arabs stop killing each other in the fight for land. To bring "Peace to Kashmir" means that Indians and Pakistanis stop fighting for control of the region. To bring "Peace to Nepal" means that the Maoists, the military, and the Nepali people will stop fighting over who will rule the country.

However, while all of the above are noble and beautiful goals, these definitions of peace are overly simplistic. Peace is not merely the absence of war. Peace is not empty space from which violence has been removed. Peace is not the passivity, which is the opposite of aggression.

Peace is full. Peace is positive. Peace is active.

Peace is a relationship or a society or a world in which there is a dynamic, constructive utilization of energy for the betterment of ourselves and each other. Peace is progress, moving further in our personal and collective evolution every day. Peace is living in harmony within ourselves and with all those with whom we share the Earth—the humans, the animals, and the plants.

It is our disharmony, our lack of connection, our lack of peace, which has resulted in waging war, polluting our Earth, turning a blind eye to the violence of poverty and injustice.

Many people think that violence and war require strategies, and that peace is passive. However, although countries and individuals who engage in violence usually plan out their attacks in advance, the compulsion to act violently is actually instinctive rather than planned. Violence is a vestigial remnant of our animal past, the crudest aspect of our lower nature, and the most destructive of our basic instincts.

Peace requires us to respond in a way that is higher and greater than our most basic, animal instinct. It requires deep thought and planning. It frequently requires us to put the greater needs of the whole over our own individual desires.

But how to reach this? How do we set aside our own desires for the greater good? How can we become so peaceful within ourselves that our peace emanates and permeates the world around us?

The answer is spirituality, whatever name or form of the Divine you follow.

Through spirituality, we begin to remove these layers that have blocked us from our true selves. In meditation, we connect back to our innermost self, calming our minds, filling our hearts with joy, bringing peace to our souls. We begin to realize the insignificance of that which causes us anxiety and troubles us, realizing the infinite joy and boundless peace that come from God and through union with our own Divine nature. In introspection, we become aware of our successes and failures, allowing ourselves to become more and more Divine, more peaceful each day. In service, we reach the essence of spirituality. As one goes deeper and deeper on a spiritual path, and as one gets closer and closer to realization and enlightenment, one realizes that the Divine resides in all. One begins to see God's presence in every person, every animal, and every plant. When one realizes this Truth deep in one's heart, one becomes filled with an insatiable desire to care for and serve all of God's creation.

When we get in touch with our internal divinity, we not only tap into the infinite well of peace within us, but we also become instruments of peace for the world.

The similarities between us far outweigh the differences, regardless of how deep or wide the chasm between us may appear. The first verse in the Ishopanishad says:

> *Isha vaasyamidam sarvam*
> *yat kincha jagatyaam jagat*
> *Tena tyaktena bhunjeethaa*
> *Maa gradhah kasya svid dhanam*

This mantra tells us that God is manifest in everything in the Universe. All is Him, and all is pervaded by Him. There is nothing which is not God.

We are all human. We all have the capacity to feel love, to feel pain, to feel fear, hunger, sadness, and joy. We all are attached to our families and want only the best for them. We all strive day after day to improve our own lives and those of our loved ones.

When we can truly cultivate these feelings of oneness in our heart, then and only then can we really begin working for lasting, unshakable peace in the world.

A multivitamin for spiritual health

It is easy to be peaceful, joyful, and calm when everything is going according to our own plan. The true test comes when God's plan runs contrary to our own.

In order to maintain inner peace, calmness, and stability regardless of external circumstances, we need a daily multivitamin of meditation, no reaction, and introspection.

Meditation

Meditation is the best medication for all agitations. Meditation calms the mind, fills the heart with joy, and brings peace to the Soul. The serenity and joy found in meditation lasts throughout the day and throughout life. Meditation is not a simple diversion, which works only as long as you are actively engaged in it. Meditation is not a pill, which quickly wears off. Rather, meditation brings you into contact with God; it changes the very nature of your being. It brings you back to the world from which you truly come: the realm of the Divine.

As you sit in meditation you will realize the insignificance of that which causes anxiety. You will realize the transient nature of all your troubles. You will realize the infinite joy and boundless peace that comes from God and through union with your own Divine nature.

Try to make a time each day that is "meditation time." It's no problem if you only have five or ten minutes. Don't worry. Just do it. Do not say, "Well, I don't have an hour to sit so I won't bother." Commit at least a few minutes to meditation each morning. Try to set time aside for meditation in a quiet, serene atmosphere. It's not crucial that mediation be for an extended period of time. What's important is that you get connected.

Then with practice, slowly you will see that your life becomes meditation. It will not be restricted to one time and place. All you will have to do is simply close your eyes, watch your breath, focus on the oneness of us all, and connect with the Divine.

You will become a torchbearer of peace, spreading the flames of serenity, love, and brotherhood wherever you go.

No reaction

After the vitamin of meditation comes the vitamin of "no reaction," which we should practice all day.

We need to learn to be calmer in our lives. We need to learn to remain still and unaffected by all that happens around us. We must learn to be like the ocean. Waves come and go, but the ocean stays. Even a large rock, thrown from a great distance with great force, will cause only temporary ripples in a small area of the surface. Most of the ocean, the depths of the ocean, will remain unaffected.

Typically, in our lives we act like the water on the surface, allowing ourselves to get tossed around by every passing wave or gust of air. We must learn to be like the calm, undisturbed water in the depths of the ocean itself, unaffected by small, transient fluctuations.

Silence time

One of the best ways to learn "no reaction" is through silence. When we are anxious, angry, tense, or frustrated, we tend to say things which we later regret; we let our words fuel the reaction in our hearts.

Let us learn the power of silence. Silence on the outside will lead to silence on the inside.

I recommend to everyone—those who are embarking on a spiritual path and those who have been treading a spiritual path for decades—to make some time each day for silence. It should not simply be time you're already silent, such as while you're sleeping or in the shower, but rather a time when you must consciously remind yourself, "I am in silence."

The practice of daily silence gets us into the habit of thinking before we speak, of remembering that—although we may have a thought—we have a choice whether to speak it out loud. This way, we become the master over our speech rather than its slave. Our words become our powerful and loyal servants, to be used when, how, and where we deem fit. We will find that we "act" more and "re-act" less.

Introspection

So, in the morning we begin with meditation. All day we practice no reaction. And at night? Introspection.

At the end of the day, a good businessman always checks his balance sheet to see how much he has earned and how much he has spent. Similarly, a good teacher reviews her students' test scores: how many passed, how many failed?

In the same way, each night we must examine the balance sheet of our day: what were our successes, what were our failures? For all the successes, all our "plus-points," we must give credit to God, for His grace and for letting us be His instruments.

Yet, our failures must also be given to God. The fault is

ours, yet we must turn these over to Him as well. We must say, "God, please take these minus points. Look at all my failures, all my minus points for even just one day. I cannot go even one day without accumulating so many minus points. But, still You love me."

In this way, each night we check our balance sheet, and we pray to God to help us have fewer minus points, to make us stronger, to make us better hands doing His work, and to give us more faith and devotion.

May there be peace to the Heavens, peace to the sky, peace to the atmosphere.
May there be peace on the Earth and peace in the waters.
May there be peace to the forests and peace to the mountains.
May there be peace to the plants, to the animals and to all creatures.
May we all live in peace. Om peace, peace, peace."
~Pujya Swamiji

About Pujya Swamiji

H.H. Pujya Swami Chidanand Saraswatiji left his home for the Himalayan jungles and forests in his early childhood, under the guidance of his spiritual master, to live a life devoted to God and in the services of humanity. Today, he is world renowned as a spiritual leader, visionary, and Divine guide.

He is President and Spiritual Head of Parmarth Niketan Ashram, one of the largest spiritual interfaith institutions in India. He has also founded and heads numerous charitable, humanitarian, and environmental organizations, including Ganga Action Parivar, Divine Shakti Foundation, India Heritage Research Foundation, and the Global Interfaith WASH Alliance.

Pujya Swamiji has been a leader in numerous international, inter-faith summits, and parliaments, including the Parliament of World Religions, the Millennium World Peace Summit at the United Nations, and the World Economic Forum. He is the recipient of innumerable awards, including the Mahatma Gandhi Humanitarian award, Hindu of the Year Award, and Best Citizens of India Award.

However, Pujya Swamiji seems unaffected by this incredible list of accomplishments and remains a pious child of God, owning nothing, draped in saffron robes, living a life of true renunciation. Thousands travel from across the globe simply to sit in his presence, to receive his "darshan." He also travels the world, bringing the Light of wisdom, inspiration, upliftment, and the Divine touch to thousands across the world.

For more information, *www.parmarth.com*

Music and Chanting
☼

By Deva Premal and Miten

*Music comes closest to meditation. Music is a way towards
meditation and the most beautiful way.*

~**Osho**

Without the silence between the notes, music is simply
noise. The silence between the notes is what makes
music so special, and that's what we have to listen for because
that's where meditation is. The rest of it is just information. If
we listen for the silence then music has the power to heal us.
The true purpose of music is to heal, not to entertain. Music
is not necessarily meant to make people forget their troubles.
Music is a bridge to the spirit. Its function is to express the
inexpressible.

Osho discovered how the power of music brings us deeper
into meditation, that music is a key that can open the door
to meditation. But we can also get stuck with the door, stuck
with the key. That's what happens to most musicians. They
become obsessed with creating the perfect key and making
it better or more intricate than others. Ego comes into the
equation and they never use the key because they're so busy
polishing it.

Miten and I honor music by using the key in a very
simple way. Our music is not sophisticated but it's totally
transformative because simplicity brings us to a space in the
heart where we are able to go beyond the mind. And that's the
real reason for music, going beyond the words, and beyond
the ego mind space. The repetition of mantra and music, with
a lot of space and silence, can create the soil for meditation.

It's our nourishment. It's what keeps us on the road. For
us, there is nothing more precious than having sung with an
audience, ecstatic with bliss, and then entering the deep silence

that the mantra brings, so deep, that with closed eyes one feels there is 'nobody' there at all. All personalities are dissolved for a tiny sacred moment and only peace remains.

Tantra-mantra

When we play music, it's the same energy for us as making love. When we play music with anyone, we stand naked—our personality, our hang ups, our fears, everything is seen. It's the same as making love and really feeling the person. That's how we approach the music. It's our tantric expression to chant these mantras together as a couple, and in that process we're uplifted and fulfilled on many levels.

Chanting mantras opens the music to totally new dimensions. It's very different than singing lyrical words, such as, "I love you baby," or "I'm so lonely today," which are emotional expressions. The mantras go deeper. We don't need to know what they mean, we just feel them. When we listen to them we're not connected to the way in which they rhyme, or to a beautiful combination of words. We're not in that place at all. Instead, we're immersed in sounds that are ancient energetic formulas.

And when you're a couple making love through the music then everything is very different. You start to see the world differently, and you see yourself differently. In fact, you see everything in a different Light. That's how the mantras can work. There's so much stress and chaos and turmoil in the world that the only thing we can offer people is a sense of inner peace. No one is going to find peace in the outer world right now. These current times are occurring to give us the opportunity to look inside and discover the bliss, the beauty, and the self-love that is our essential nourishment. And that's what the mantras give you.

The mystery of the mantra

We started putting music to mantras twenty-three years ago, creating holistic chants that contain energy. Every sound has a certain effect on our energetic bodies. If we close our eyes and say or sing 'ahhh' for ten minutes, it has a totally different feeling than if we say or sing 'oooh' or 'ummmm' for ten minutes. As a result, we're drawn to one sound more than another.

There were ancient wise men and women in India who were able to pull these sounds from the beyond and give voice to them. Out of that emerged the Sanskrit language, which is an energy based sound language rather than meaning based. Energy based means that every sound is the equivalent of the manifestation. For example, when you say or sing the word 'prema,' which is 'love.' It's not something that points to love, it is the sound vibration of the feeling and essence of love. It's totally direct and everyone understands it because it's cellular; it goes straight to the core of every human being.

Every Sanskrit word has a completely different energetic quality, and that's what the mantras bring to life. That's why there are so many mantras that can help us tune into the varying aspects of life and the beyond.

In the Vedas they say we have seventy-two thousand Nadis that are energy lines in our body, rather like meridians. 'Nad' means 'sound.' The energy lines are there for the sound current to move through. When we chant a mantra one-hundred and eight times, the sound current washes through our being, through our energetic bodies, and through our physical bodies, transforming us on all levels—body, mind, and spirit.

Playing an instrument and singing as meditation

In Indian music, when you learn any instrument you also learn to sing the notes you're playing. You introduce the quality of the human voice to join your instrument. The voice carries the emotion and the space of the person. It's a very direct experience.

Also, it is impossible to hide with your voice. If you're upset when you sing everyone will know that you're upset. When we sing we focus on the out-breath, and we consciously let the breath go to the end of our capacity. But the most beautiful thing is that when people sing together, they all breathe together because they're all engaged in the same rhythm of in breath and out breath.

Being in meditation basically being means absorbed in whatever you're doing, being in the moment, and not being distracted or half-hearted. Music is an amazing mirror in that way. You can really feel when you space out, and then you can come back to the music and the breath.

Music associated with memories

Music is the art which is most nigh to tears and memory (Oscar Wilde). Music and songs generally create an emotional connection, or nostalgia. Music evokes certain times and moments in our lives because it stirs the particular emotion we were feeling at that time, especially love songs.

Mantras aren't emotion based, so they don't have that same emotional trigger as most ordinary songs do. Once you absorb the mantra it's not something that leaves you and then comes back; it stays with you forever. It's not something in the past. It comes out of the present and it lives in the present. It's a different thing than when you're being nostalgic or feeling sad or remembering a particular moment. Mantras are beyond the emotional plane. They talk about a deeper love, way beyond our human 'I love you.' And so when you become friends with a mantra, it's nothing to do with emotion. It carries you through your whole life. Mantras keep you connected. If you chant all day, then you'll be connected all day.

Celestial sounds

We can discover celestial sounds by listening instead of hearing. Mostly we don't listen to the sound of the wind or the sound of birds singing. We might hear them outside chirping away, but we don't really feel the beauty and the joy and the total freedom of the bird, or the spirit of the wind blowing, so we have to be tuned in to hear celestial sounds.

I'm most aware of celestial sounds at the start of each concert we play. We begin with silence, so it takes the audience a while to shuffle after applauding us. Then they shuffle some more, and we sit there in silence until eventually everyone goes absolutely quiet. Then there is the possibility for celestial sound to come in.

At that time, Deva chants a mantra and from that moment we have a celestial sound because we're all open and listening. We're not hearing accidentally; we're in the moment and we're receptive. Everyone listening together makes the energy more profound. We become one energy, one breath, and when we sing we don't think about breathing. The music literally breathes us. We take the same breaths more or less at the same time, and we all fall into synchronicity with each other. Suddenly we're all chanting and we all feel as one without knowing why. And that's when the celestial sounds happen.

When the people in the audience are receptive for this experience, and we are all joined as one, it is beautiful for us and it nourishes us so much. When we tap into this space of celestial sound and silence, it's like making love every night.

> *There's music in the sighing of a reed;*
> *There's music in the gushing of a rill;*
> *There's music in all things, if men had ears:*
> *Their Earth is but an echo of the spheres.*
> **~Lord Byron**

It's very easy to open up to sound. Firstly, we have to stop doing whatever we're doing. We have to slow down, keep slowing down, and then find a place to stop. It takes a while to sit without movement and breathe. Then listen. If we focus on these three things then we will be very aware of celestial sounds and music.

Imagine yourself as the center of the Universe with a 5.1 surround sound system, hearing all these different sounds happening in space. It's totally multi-dimensional, and every sound can help us to come back into the moment. Every sound can be a tuning into meditation.

Meditation is always about, 'How I can be in the moment? How can I be totally here and now?' The sounds are always here and now because they happen when they happen, so each sound can be an anchor into the present moment. It's beautiful to feel that each sound is part of a symphony, rather than a disturbance, so when a car passes by we can feel that without judgment.

Sometimes it also helps to imagine that we are listening from the belly rather than the ears, because the belly is not connected to the brain like the ears are. That way you can hear the sounds for what they are, and you don't put so much judgment on whether they are beautiful or not. Rather, you take each sound as a gift and a pointer to the present moment. It's a beautiful way to be a part of God's symphony. It's only possible to listen to that when we slow down, when we reach the point of realizing, 'I'm sitting here doing nothing, eyes closed, and all I can do without those senses is to hear, listen, breathe.' Then we can notice the sounds around us.

These are the keys into our own inner sanctum, our own inner peace. We're literally making friends with our own inner world, becoming relaxed and comfortable with ourselves with no external diversion. When we do that for long enough we'll find a love for who we really are inside, and that's where it gets exciting and interesting.

Music playing itself

If the music that accompanies the mantras is nice and enjoyable to sing to, then the music stays within. You could be shopping in a supermarket and chanting a mantra for compassion without even realizing you're doing it. If the mantras bubble up inside you when you're driving to work, for example, then you're blessed. That's why we put music to the mantras, and use sensitive musicians to do it, so that the mantras stay with us.

Many people tell us they have used the mantras for life-changing events, such as bringing a baby into the world or supporting a beloved one as they transition from their body. But they also carry mantras with them into everyday activities. If you're feeling blocked or stuck, or beginning a new adventure, a new job, or a new relationship you'd want the Ganesh mantra with you as it supports the removing of obstacles. Each mantra and the energy of the sounds will carry you in a certain way.

Once you make friends with the mantra and it starts to get in your blood, you'll walk around chanting it without even realizing it. You literally become the vibration of it. It's definitely more beneficial than most of the thoughts that go through our head!

Deva's story

I was born in Germany. When my mother was pregnant with me, my parents' welcome was to sing the Gayatri Mantra throughout the pregnancy. As I grew up, we continued to chant the Gayatri Mantra together regularly before bed. I didn't know what I was singing, or why. I just did it because I was told to! It wasn't until much later in life that I came to appreciate these precious times and what my parents wanted to give me.

As a teenager, I moved away from the confines of both my classical music training in voice, violin, and piano, and the mantra practice, and began to explore on my own. At the age of 11 life brought me to Osho, who gave me the name 'Deva Premal,' which means Divine loving in Sanskrit.

In Osho's ashram I met Miten. Although I was 20-years-old and he was 42, our hearts immediately connected. I knew Miten was one of Osho's musicians, but that was about all I knew, apart from the fact that I felt good whenever we met. We laughed a lot, and we still do now.

Miten's story

I was born in London and grew up in the sixties. At that time, England was alive with rock and roll music and the sound of The Beatles. It was a time of innocence, when you could sense the possibility that life has no boundaries. I later established a successful career as a singer/songwriter, touring with bands such as Fleetwood Mac, Lou Reed, and Ry Cooder. During this time I released two albums, one produced by The Kinks, another by noted Los Angeles producer, Bones Howe. This period of my life was certainly exciting, but it left me feeling spiritually unfulfilled. I was looking for something more substantial in my life than the prescribed diet of sex, drugs, and rock and roll.

I read a book of discourses on Zen, by Osho, and had an epiphany, which led me to leave everything I'd known before. I sold my guitars and travelled to Osho to begin a new life as the member of a community that had gathered around him. Here I found a new approach to music.

It was an amazing revelation. I wasn't prepared for the healing power that music contained. This turned my head to what sacred music was; a mixture of eastern and western in style; uplifting and spiritual in nature. I became hooked on a meditation known as 'Sufi Dance,' and never missed an opportunity to participate. All this music, along with a life of communal integration, deeper relating, and Osho's stimulating discourses and meditations, healed me from whatever wounds I'd been carrying around music and life in general. After I met Osho, everything fell into place. He gave purpose to my life, and an understanding that Divine chaos is the essence of it. My eyes were opened to new possibilities, which I continue to explore to this day.

When I met Deva, I was coordinating the ashram music, taking responsibility for all the evening musical meditations in which thousands of people participated. Eventually I invited Deva to join, which began our musical and intimate partnership.

One day, some years later, we were in England participating in a music festival when we heard the Gayatri Mantra being chanted. As she knew the sounds so well, Deva immediately reconnected with the mantra and after that we began featuring it in our concerts.

We began searching out more mantras and soon had enough for our first album, which was recorded in Deva's mother's apartment in Germany, where she was born, and where the Gayatri Mantra had been chanted continually all those years before. Our objective was to make an album for friends who attended our workshops and who needed music for their massage sessions. We gave it the title, The Essence. We never expected a great outcome, so how it was received went beyond our wildest dreams. We were soon receiving floods of orders, and having to continually replenish stock.

Light Practice

The best way that we know to reconnect with the Light of the Divine is to chant mantras. Here are a few of our favorites:

The Gayatri Mantra is the mantra that began with the beginning of the Universe. It's the oldest and most frequently chanted mantra, and the one Deva grew up with as a child. It's a prayer to the sun and it goes like this:

Om bhur bhuvaha svaha
Tat savitur varenyam
Bhargo devasya dhimahi
Dhiyo yonah prachodayat

Om is another favorite. Om is the sound of eternity and the Universe. It's the soundless sound. It's so vast that it's impossible to describe it. It's related to the sixth chakra, which is the third eye chakra.

Here are some other mantras you can chant to transform your life:

Om Shreem Mahalakshmiyei Namaha
- abundance in all forms

Om Gum Ganapatayei Namaha
- remover of obstacles

Om Eim Saraswatyei Swaha
- success in creative endeavors

Om Namah Shivaya
- opening to Divine consciousness

Music is a bridge to the Spirit.
~Deva Premal and Miten

About Deva Premal and Miten

Deva Premal and Miten's worldwide concerts and best-selling albums have introduced millions of westerners to the joy and deep relaxation found in spiritually based songs and chanting mantras from the eastern meditation traditions.

Their debut album, The Essence, which rocketed to the top of New Age charts around the world when it was released in 1998, introduced a unique musical genre, offering the ancient mantras of India and Tibet in contemporary musical settings.

Since then Deva and Miten have released a string of acclaimed CDs with sales exceeding one million, and their concerts have moved from yoga studios to audiences of thousands in concert halls, cathedrals, and music festivals around the planet.

Their music transcends all the usual boundaries, receiving accolades from such luminaries as Eckhart Tolle, who calls their music "pure magic," to His Holiness the Dalai Lama who is reported to enjoy their music during his private time.

For more information, *www.DevaPremalMiten.com*

Abundance and Detachment

By Terry Tillman

Having rests on giving, and not on getting.
~**Course in Miracles**

A lot of people say they want success but they haven't questioned how they define and measure success. In western, capitalistic, materialistic cultures success is usually measured objectively, such as how big is my bank account, how many properties do I have, what's my net worth? Anybody who goes down that trail eventually realizes that's not a very good definition of success.

When I was in my early thirties I had all the trappings that people call success. I had six businesses, property, a vacation home, an airplane, and more. But inside I was bankrupt and I was afraid to tell anybody. I thought, *I did everything I was taught, and this is it? I'm not happy and I don't know what to do about it.*

I look back on that 15 year period after college as the black hole of my life, and one important thing I learned was that's not how you measure success. You don't only measure success objectively, at a deeper level you measure it subjectively—do I have more than the symbols of success? Do I have the experience of success I really want? Am I happy? Do I have joy? Do I have peace of mind? Do I have loving in my life? All of these are invisible things. The more we have those invisible things, the more abundant we are. True abundance is not material possessions. I went after the symbol thinking it would give me the experience. *If I just had more money then I'd be secure. If I had a longer vacation then I would relax.* I thought if I just got the symbol—the thing—then that would give me what I really wanted, which is the experience of the inner invisible stuff. I figured out that I was doing it backwards. Most of us learned that if we just have more money, a better business, a new car, a house…whatever it is…then we will be doing what we want, and then we will be happy, secure, successful, joyful, loving. That's backwards. What works is to first answer, who am I? And from that will naturally flow something to do. And then we will have whatever is needed to support who we are. That's how the Universe is designed. But it takes a lot of trust and faith to do that—until you have that experience and then you will know. I know this to be true because I've gone through it several times; the hard way and also the way that works. I'm not always in the knowing, but I'll never forget that there is such a place because it is part of my experience. I've gone from being a very wealthy young man with a lot of assets, but a lack of the invisible stuff inside, to experiencing all the way to the other side of the spectrum, where I have little materially, yet I feel very rich and abundant. I may not have money in the bank, but I have a loving relationship, clothes on my back, shelter, good food, and I'm at peace most of the time.

The Law of Abundance

I have a degree from Stanford in Economics. Economics is known as 'the dismal science' for a reason. The first law of economics is also called the Law of Scarcity, and all subsequent economic theory is based on that. However, the first law is not true. There's a bigger, higher spiritual law working in the Universe called the Law of Abundance, which is about a cycle of giving and receiving. When this cycle is uninterrupted and flows freely, the natural, automatic, guaranteed result is abundance. Many people are familiar with this as, "being in the flow."

At the source of the Jordan River in Israel, water comes out of the ground and it flows south until it reaches the Sea of Galilee. The Sea of Galilee is a great big lake environment that's abundant. There's agriculture all around, there's fishing, there's tourism, it's pretty, and the Christian history is centered there. Then the water exits the south end of the Sea of Galilee and flows until it reaches the Dead Sea. Do you know why it's called the "Dead Sea?" There's no organic biological life there. It has a lack of abundance in the ways we'd usually define that. Why? It has no outlet, so it receives but it does not give back. This natural flow of giving and receiving is blocked, and when there's a blockage, abundance disappears.

We see similar examples throughout nature—cycles of plants through the seasons, reproduction cycle of salmon, animals... pick any part of nature and you can notice how it's interconnected and the natural design is abundance. If that is interrupted lack and scarcity begin to show up. This is the primary cause of the environmental problems we're experiencing today. If we can learn to come into cooperation with the way it's designed, then life will be far easier.

I do a wilderness trip in Idaho most years and we begin at a place called Red Fish Lake. It's the most inland spawning ground for the salmon and it's 1400 miles from the Pacific ocean, so to get there the salmon go up the Columbia River, up the Snake River, up the Salmon River, and into Red Fish Creek and the lake where they spawn. The first time I saw this during spawning season, 40 years ago, I couldn't see the bottom of Red Fish Creek as there were so many fish. Twelve years ago one fish made it back to Red Fish Lake. The natural flow had been interrupted by dams on the rivers, agriculture chemicals, fertilizers, pesticides, over-fishing, and so on. The cycle was broken and as a result, it affected everything. In 2008, 602 salmon made it back because the blocks in the cycle had started to be removed—some dams were breached, some farmers stopped using toxic fertilizers and pesticides (which leach into the rivers), and better fish ladders and screens were constructed around dams.

Unblocking giving and receiving

When the cycle is flowing freely the automatic result is abundance, but we block the energetic flow of giving and receiving, mainly through our attitude and belief systems. For example, many people are afraid of losing what they have so they hang onto it. That blocks the giving and stops the flow. There's a part of them that thinks there's not enough or that they have it now but they might not be able to get it again, so they become attached and fearful. This creates a blockage. In order to become unblocked they need to learn how to let go and detach.

Many people learn about tithing through their churches... that's an effective way to start letting go, detaching, and recognizing that there's a bigger source. Also, it's important to acknowledge that in a grander Truth we don't actually own anything. Legally we may have title to our property, but from a higher perspective, we don't own it, we just get to use it. We're the custodians, but at some point we will be separated from it, either at our death or before.

The indigenous populations have always taught this important Truth. Most American Indians hold a pow-wow once a year, which is a celebration where they feast, sing, dance, and bring gifts to give away and share. The member who gives away the most is considered the wealthiest. That's the opposite of most western cultures. We think that the one who collects and accumulates the most is the wealthiest, but from a higher spiritual perspective the one who gives the most is the wealthiest and is the one who also opens up to greater levels of abundance.

In this Abundance cycle we can choose to be either a small trickle or a great big Amazon River. The Amazon River gives as much as it receives, but it couldn't give if it didn't also receive. Most people who are blocked on the receiving side don't feel worthy of receiving. The best way I know to unblock the receiving side is through the practice of gratitude. I finish my day by writing down everything I'm grateful for. Gratitude works on both sides of the cycle of giving and receiving. The moment we're grateful, we're abundant. We could be starving, own no property, and have no money in our pocket yet we could look around and find something we're grateful for—the air we breathe, sunshine, rain, beautiful scenery, good friends, our senses, nose, mouth, eyes, legs, experience…and in that instant we're abundant.

The experience of abundance is more important than the symbol of abundance. The symbol will never give us the experience. I might go and buy a brand new suit and the first day I wear it I feel really cool. The next time I wear it, I might feel okay, but after four or five times of wearing it the feeling changes and it becomes just clothing. It isn't the clothes that give us the experience, it's our response to them. It isn't what happens out there, it's our inner response to what happens out there that creates the experience.

In the past I was proud to call myself an accumulator. For a period of time I'd look at my balance sheet every day to see if it had increased. I was really good at receiving, but I wasn't very good at giving back out. I was stingy. I was afraid of losing it. I was afraid I couldn't make any more. I realized I needed to go to work on sharing and giving. Initially I started small, tipping 20 percent instead of 10 to 15 percent in restaurants, leaving change with the vendor, paying for friend's meals. I started giving money away and donating when I thought I couldn't. I knew I had to get rid of my sense of lack.

In order to get more you need to give more. Here's a cool awareness I eventually had: when the cycle of abundance is unblocked there's no difference between giving and receiving. It's the same. You give something and you're rewarded simply by the giving.

Learning detachment

In 1982 I built two homes in my dream location in Ketchum, Idaho, home of the first destination ski resort in the USA, Sun Valley. The homes were on a creek, across from a golf course, at the base of a world famous ski mountain—location, location, location! I planned to sell one and keep the other. But then the prime interest rate hiked up to 22 percent. The country entered a severe real estate depression. I had a construction loan a per cent above prime, a very large loan on about five million dollars worth of property, and I found myself selling almost everything else to keep paying the mortgage debt.

After about three years of this I called the bank and said, "Take it, it's yours." I surrendered, detached, and let go. My balance sheet went way down, but for that tuition I learned detachment, one of the most valuable lessons of my life. I learned that all suffering comes from attachment and that surrendering, letting go, detaching, accepting, cooperating are all keys to joy, happiness, and peace of mind. The worst thing I could imagine happened to me and I felt free. It's like I took their worst shot (whoever the imagined enemy *they* are) and it didn't hurt that bad.

I still go through the moments of doubt, concern, and fear but don't stay there. A day would be a long time. When things don't happen the way I want them to, I ask, "What if this is for me?" I've always found that it is almost always better than had it gone my way.

Receiving and worthiness

My solution to bankruptcy inside was closing six businesses and going to work for Lifespring, one of the first Human Potential seminar companies. On the first two days of a five-day advanced seminar people were exposed to their limiting character and survival behaviors, and for the rest of the seminar we supported participants to connect to who they really are in the heart. That was a magnificent and beautiful experience.

One time I was facilitating a five-day training in Seattle, Washington. There was a son of an Indian Chief in the course who was denying his heritage and ashamed he was an Indian. He went by the name of Carl. I asked him to do a sun dance, but he refused, thinking I was humiliating him. The entire fourth day of the seminar was centered around an improvisational theater technique. One by one people would be in front of the room sharing and being who they essentially are, metaphorically transforming from a caterpillar to a butterfly. They'd be their limiting self and then they'd transform into something magnificent. They would be it. They couldn't just act it, theorize it, talk about it or pretend. We'd work with them until they were 100 percent there.

In those days we assigned people a stretch, encouraging them to commit fully and go 100 percent, from the inside out. I told Carl to finish with a sun dance. When he left for the day he was so resistant that I wasn't sure he'd return the next day. He did.

On the day there was a palpable energy in the room. The young Indian walked into the room wearing full ceremonial regalia…white leather pants, a jacket with fringes and jewels, and an eagle feather headdress that went to the floor. He was regal, and all heads turned and mouths dropped open upon his entrance. When it was his turn he first announced that his true name was Yellow Wolf, and then he did an authentic sun dance—breathtaking, stunning, and magical.

We were in a room with floor to ceiling windows and curtains. On one end I had the windows open to let some air in as it was stuffy in the room. He finished in front of the room, looking toward the Heavens with his arms stretched out like a cross. I was standing to the side where I could see him as well as all the participants facing him. I had my back to the windows. All of a sudden I noticed everyone's eyes open wide and mouths drop open. I turned to see what they were startled by. One curtain over only one of the four windows had blown open 45 degrees and stayed there for what seemed like a minute (but was probably about 15 seconds) before gently closing.

Yellow Wolf noticed everyone looking, turned, glancing over his shoulder, then turned back and said, "Where I come from that is the Great Spirit. He is with us now." Then he walked over to me and took a ring off his finger and said, "This was given to me by my father, Chief Flying Eagle. It was given to my father by my grandfather, Chief White Horse. My grandfather received it from my great grandfather. When it was given to me I was told to add to it and pass it on, and that I would know when it's time." He took off the ring and handed it to me.

I was thinking, *I can't take this. It's something so valuable, you can't give that to me. This has got tradition, it's your tribe, it's your family. It belongs to chiefs. You're a chief. I'm not.* And then I heard my grandmother's voice, "Sometimes the greatest gift you can give to another is to allow them to give to you." So I took a tearful breath and received it. He said, "It's yours now to add to and pass along and you will know when it's time."

The gift he gave me was greater than the ring. I've walked through my life with the knowing that somewhere in my future is that person. And I can't begin to tell you what that positive possibility, which has never left me, has meant to me.

Wanting

People often ask me why they don't get more of the things they want. The answer is simple. The hidden reason why you don't have what you say you want is because you want it. Huh? When I want something it means I don't have it, and like attracts like, so when I say I want something I'm coming from a place of lack. There's a part of my energy, vibration, resonation that's going to resonate with lack, and that's what's going to show up in my life. Scientists and musicians call it sympathetic vibration. Anything with the same frequency and vibration inherent will be attracted and resonate in kind. This is most commonly noticed with stringed instruments and is equally as true metaphysically with people's energy.

In the late sixties there was a bestselling book about the

care and nurturing of plants. It said that indoor plants would thrive and grow when they had pleasant music around them or loving people as they literally responded to the loving emotion. To test this, a scientist took a simple life form, a vat of yoghurt, and connected it to sensitive recording equipment, similar to an EEG, and then performed different actions around the yoghurt. He played various genres of music, and the yoghurt responded with corresponding unique waves. Then he brought people in. A couple was affectionate with each other and the instrument recorded loving waves. Then people started arguing, and the instrument recorded arguing waves. No matter what the stimulus, the yoghurt responded with different wave patterns on the recording equipment.

Then the scientist divided the vat of yoghurt in half and put one vat in a room down the hall and connected it with the same type of recording equipment, but no people present. In the first room he repeated the experiment—classical music, classical waves, rock music, rock waves, loving behavior, loving waves. An instant later in the other empty room the instrument recorded the same wave patterns as in the first room. This demonstrated that there is a measurable vibrational connection between what seems to be disconnected physical objects and it's true with anything on the planet, not just yoghurt.

More recently, the Japanese scientist Masuro Emoto showed that words written on containers of water effect the cellular, crystalline pattern of the water. And also recently two Russian scientists proved that the vibration in what people say to each other effects the genetic and DNA formation in both the person being spoken to and the person speaking.

The above story is an example of where we look is where we go. What we focus on, think about, and look at determines the vibrational pattern inside of us. Most people identify it as a feeling or an emotion, which is the result of the focus. What we say to ourselves, think about, and imagine effects our vibration, as does what the people in our environment focus on. So if I watch news channels that are predominantly negative that negativity goes into my system and affects my health and wellbeing.

Abundance doesn't only mean financial abundance; it's the abundance of anything. We could have the abundance of sickness, negative thoughts, joy, happiness, positive experiences. We could have a lot of anything and that's determined by our focus and the environment we place ourselves in. We need to focus on what we want more of rather when what we want less of.

So if we want to be more abundant we have to focus on, think about, and tell ourselves abundant things, and surround ourselves with uplifting, positive, abundant surroundings. We need to create an environment we want and feel good in. That includes the physical surroundings as well as people.

How can people lead more abundant lives?

To apply the experience of greater abundance in our lives we need to set up structures and systems that support the positive focus, and what we want more of. The most common way is through affirmations, which are personal, positive, present tense statements. They work because they change our focus, which changes our vibration. The cool thing about affirmations is that we don't need to believe them in order for them to work. We just need to do them repeatedly, over an extended period until they become unconscious. Also, we need to put ourselves in a positive environment. It's not a good idea to spend time with people who are constantly negative, complaining, and unhappy. This may mean we're no longer around certain people, including family and friends. Instead, spend time with people who intend to be positive. We have a responsibility to take care of ourselves first.

Create a vision board by collecting images of things you want in your future and stick them on a piece of card. You can also add specific screensavers to your computer and subscribe to magazines with images based on the topic of what you want more of. I'm subscribed to two travel magazines, which are full of images and articles on travel. I've been looking at those magazines for 35 years as it holds my focus on what I love and want. In 1978 I lived in Pacific Heights in San Francisco, the most expensive neighborhood in USA. Three of us roomed together and shared the rent. Being there and seeing the surrounding mansions, and the beautiful view of San Francisco Bay and Golden Gate Bridge in my daily environment, was the best vision board I've ever had.

Belief systems

We tend to have the most limiting beliefs around money, such as 'it takes hard work to make money,' 'money doesn't grow on trees,' 'money is the root of all evil,' 'it's easier for a camel to pass through the eye of the needle than a rich man to enter the Kingdom of Heaven.'

For example, if we take the belief, 'it takes hard work to make money,' I don't want hard in my life, so if I believe it takes hard work to make money then I'm going to stay away from money. If my intention is to have more money, if I believed money was good and I deserved it, then I'd have more. But if I have a belief that says money is the root of all evil then a part of my consciousness will go away from money, resulting in either no money or less money, because I don't want evil. We have hundreds of unconscious beliefs. It's important to know that beliefs are not necessarily true. Yet, we go through our life believing they are true and act accordingly.

I could take any belief someone has and show them a contrary point of view that's just as valid or that would eliminate the negative belief. For example, 'money is the root of all evil' comes out the Bible. It must be true, God's word after all. But that's not really what it says…it says, 'The lust after money is the root of all evil, not the money itself.' It's lust that leads to evil and problems, not money. In my seminars I go through many of these beliefs, changing them by demonstrating the true meanings. New information, new belief. Then we need to eliminate it and clear it from our unconscious and physiology. There are techniques for doing this. The information is easily available on the internet. Best though is to is to find a good live seminar or coach.

Light Practice

Find something that has value to you and give it away... let it go...detach.

Conclusion

The more people accumulate in the physical world, the more difficult it is for them to let go of that. Things and stuff won't give us happiness. Very often the more we accumulate the less happy we tend to be.

The cycle of giving and receiving is not new. Some of the ways people recognize this are through sayings such as, 'as you sow so you reap,' 'as you give, you're given unto to,' 'what goes around comes around.'

It's the willingness to let go completely, that moves us into the flow and results in more. The giving must be unconditional with no strings attached—if it has strings attached they must only be heart strings.

For me it's reduced inside to a knowing and that has always required a lot of trust and faith. My goal is to have that knowing live in me so I don't need the trust and the faith, and from there the unconditional giving becomes easier and so does the flow. Whatever I let go of, there will always be more.

You can never have something until you let it go. Until then it has you.

~**Terry Tillman**

About Terry Tillman

Terry Tillman has hosted engaging, inspiring, life-changing personal development and leadership seminars since 1977. He has worked in ninety-eight countries to help people find their life purpose and connect with their true Self.

Terry often calls himself a recovered businessman. Once a Type A workaholic, he turned his life around after being introduced to the world of transformational education. More dramatic change occurred after an accident in which doctors told him he would never walk again. Nine months later Terry proved them wrong and today he is as fit and healthy as ever.

Nowadays, Terry works with a select number of companies and individuals who seek excellent results and he teaches self-development in the wilderness of Idaho. His book about peace, *The Writings on the Wall*, was an international bestseller. His next book, *The Call*™ is coming soon.

For more information, *www.227company.com*

Money and Spirituality

By Joe Vitale

The sole purpose of money is to express appreciation.
~Arnold Patent

M oney.

We use it, abuse it, let it distort us and confuse us. Yet money is just paper and ink, or metal and imprint. It's nothing until someone says it's something. And by the time we are conscious enough to know it's meaningful in some way to our survival, we are programmed to believe it's more than what objective reality knows. Money ends up controlling us—or, more specifically, we are controlled by our perceptions of it.

What gives?

Money is a symbol of spiritual energy. It reveals who we are without changing itself. It's the perfect mirror. Money in the hands of a person run by their lower thoughts is a tool for destruction. Money in the hands of a highly spiritual person is a tool to make their life mission come true. But it's not the money. It's the person handling it. Money simply reflects their beliefs.

The irony in all this is we all have programming about money, whether we are spiritual or not. The spiritual person thinks money is bad and tries to live without it. Yet thinking it's bad is a judgment that a truly spiritual person wouldn't have. Thinking money is bad is proof of a lack of spirituality, not of spirituality. In other words, since money is really neutral energy, someone judging it as bad is revealing their limited view of objective reality, and denying themselves their own good. As Albert Camus wrote, "It's a kind of spiritual snobbery that makes people think they can be happy without money."

On the opposite side of the coin, so to speak, we have wealthy people with no spirituality. They think money is the be-all and end-all of life. In their pursuit of more money, they sell their Soul and lose their connection to the essence of life. They believe money has power, or can give it. They have given away their own ability to choose balance and wholeness in life in pursuit of the dollar. They think money is scarce and they fight, deceive, and compete to have it. They believe what comedian Henny Youngman said: "I've got all the money I'll ever need if I die by four o'clock."

Both, of course, are coming from belief systems that are controlling them rather than awakening them. The spiritual person who renounces money has beliefs that, "Money is evil" or, "Money corrupts." The wealthy person has beliefs, too, such as "Money is power," "Spirituality is weak," or "Greed is good." Obviously, beliefs around money control whether you have it or not. Think it's bad and you'll push it away. Think it's good and you'll attract it. Money has no beliefs about you. But you have plenty about money. Change the beliefs and you can welcome money.

But we have to go deeper than that observation. We have to have a knowing about the spirituality of money. We need to be free of beliefs that blind us or limit us. We need to make peace with money and know it can be a source of Light, too.

How do we do that?

I've discovered that we have intentions and counter-intentions. Most people have heard of intentions. That's where you state what you want to have, do, or be. It's a declaration, an affirmation, a command. Examples might be: "I intend to have more money," or "I intend to increase my sales by 25 percent." Sounds good, right?

But few know about counter-intentions. The counter-intention denies or vetoes the intention. Examples might be:

"Money is a poison," or "Money is in short supply," or "Money goes to everyone else but me."

While the conscious intention is clear and positive, the unconscious counter-intention overrides it. Until you get clear of the counter-intentions, achieving stated intentions will be difficult to impossible.

Why?

Simply put, the conscious mind has little power; the unconscious/subconscious is the driver. Our beliefs, mindset, memories, and more are stored in the subconscious/unconscious. It's the control center for most of our life. Trying to redirect our lives consciously won't work well if we have counter-intentions blocking their fulfillment. We need to get clear to get the results we prefer.

If you want to attract more money, you need to be internally at peace with money. Almost everyone has the belief, "Money is the root of all evil." If that belief remains, you'll struggle with money. After all, who wants something evil in their life? But when you question the belief, and discover it's from the longer Biblical phrase, "The love of money is the root of all evil," you can then realize that money can be yours if you don't fall in love with it. You have a new knowing about money.

Arnold Patent provided clarity here. He wrote in his little book, *Money*, the following: "The sole purpose of money is to express appreciation." Let that sink in. When you write a check for your utilities, be grateful you have them. When you write a check for your car payment, be grateful you have transportation. Money isn't about love. It's about gratitude. Start thinking of money in a state of thankfulness and you won't fall in love with it, but you will appreciate it.

Besides the change of mindset, another way to attract more money is to give it away. It sounds counter-intuitive. But tithing and other concepts of giving have been around for centuries. The idea of giving ten percent of your income to wherever you received spiritual nourishment is ancient. But it's more than religious or philosophical. It's psychological, too.

When you give, you send a signal to your mind that you

are wealthy enough to share. Plus, you are stepping into the knowing of spiritual wealth. You are showing yourself and the world that you have more than enough, and you have the faith that more is coming. Looked at another way, the window you receive through is made bigger by the window you give through. Give more, receive more.

Following your passion

But giving and beliefs aren't the only players in this dance of money, and you, knowing, and spirituality. Following your passion is key. When people pursue profit, they often do it to only make a buck. There's little connection to their life mission or Soul's purpose. While there's nothing wrong with making money, it's far more natural and energizing to make it doing what you love. Passion seems to be the ticket to profit.

As Walt Disney once said, "I want to make money from my movies so I can continue making movies." It wasn't money for greed, or money to be great; it was money for completing a spiritual mission. In Walt's case, the mission was making movies. He had a knowing about his spiritual calling, and that, combined with making peace with money, enabled him to attract it. It was a tool for his mission.

Following your passion doesn't guarantee immediate success. Most successes, including great wealth, have to be grown into. People who win the lotto and aren't prepared mentally to handle a sudden flush of cash, lose it. They unconsciously sabotage their own success. But all of the perceived failures of life are just incoming feedback to help us correct our course.

A billionaire once said he learned a great deal from failure in business. "Nothing bad happens to you," he explained. "The world forgets and forgives. You are to learn from any perceived failure, treat it as feedback, and adjust your next moves accordingly." In short, you have a knowing that what others call failure is actually just course correction on your spiritual adventure through life. It's part of the program to awaken.

I went from homeless to poverty to today living the lifestyle of the rich and famous. I pursued my passion of being an author even when I had no car, no home, no income, and no lunch money. I read in the public library. I studied on my own. I kept writing. My "overnight" success took thirty years. But those decades were the fine-tuning I needed to correct my belief system and learn my skills. Today, I'm an author with over 50 books, and a musician with over 15 albums. Following my passion led and lit the way, but I still needed to do the spiritual work of raising my own consciousness and preparing for my own success.

The awakened millionaire

Today I teach people to become what I call Awakened Millionaires. This is the new breed of humankind where money and spirituality merge in peace and lead to life and planetary transformation. Along the way, and explained in my book, *The Awakened Millionaire*, I found a set of key principles that I call The Awakened Millionaire's Creed:

• The Awakened Millionaire are driven first by their passion, purpose, and mission
• The Awakened Millionaire uses money as a Soulful tool to make a positive impact
• The Awakened Millionaire is persistently empowered, believing in themselves absolutely
• The Awakened Millionaire is committed to grow, improve, reinvent, and always discover
• The Awakened Millionaire is unshakably bold, takes risks, and does not hesitate
• The Awakened Millionaire is guided by the Soulful resonance of their intuition
• The Awakened Millionaire knows wealth is everything they have, not just money
• The Awakened Millionaire holds a deep gratitude for all they have and achieve

• The Awakened Millionaire is permanently connected to Universal abundance
• The Awakened Millionaire is generous, ethical, and focuses on the good of others
• The Awakened Millionaire champions the win-win-win
• The Awakened Millionaire Soulfully shares their entrepreneurial gifts
• The Awakened Millionaire leads by example as the catalyst for transformation in others.

A key idea to grasp is the difference between being a victim or a victor. Many people say, "It is what it is." That's a statement of victim mentality. It's what people say when they feel they can't change anything. But a spiritually empowered person realizes there are no limits and no impossibilities, whether pursuing money or enlightenment. They have a knowing that their inner connection to life is their spiritual GPS to success.

I often wear a T-shirt I made with the new phrase I coined: "It is what you accept." Anyone wanting to change their bank account needs to understand that the power to do so is in his or her hands. It isn't, "It is what it is" but instead, "It is what you accept." You may decide to accept some things as inevitable, such as the death of a loved one, but at least you have the knowing that you accepted it. You didn't give the power to another. You made the decision internally. It gives you more power to know the decision was yours. It's the same with money. You get what you accept.

Taking action

Another key principle concerns action. Too many people sit and wait for money to materialize in front of them. I believe in magic and miracles, and unexpected income, but I also believe your role in the process of attracting money is to actually do something to bring it your way. Act on your ideas. Now. "Money likes speed" is my favorite mantra. It lights an urgency inside you to motivate you forward. Life is a co-creation and you have your part to do to bring your spiritual directives into concrete form.

If you don't act now, you'll see your idea manifested in a store some day and somebody else will be attracting money from it. Recently, I read about the beginnings of the electric car. Apparently, so many people received the idea of creating an electric car at all about the same time but in different countries, that no one person is credited with building the first one. The Universe/Great Spirit knows most people don't act on their inspirations, so It gives the same idea to several people. When you receive an idea, jump on it. Bring it into being. Know that it is a gift. Know that it is a chance for you to prosper. Know that spirit is helping you and now expects you to act on the idea.

What can you do right now, today, to move toward creating something that will attract more money? Whatever it is, do it. When you doubt and second-guess yourself instead of taking action, you are demonstrating that you aren't yet clear about your intentions or clear of counter-intentions about money and your right to attract it. Act now. Follow inspiration, which is the Light of knowing from within.

Acting despite fear is also key. Fear is of the ego; faith is knowing from spirit. I've learned that your wealth is hiding under the very thing you fear. In other words, do the thing and you'll have the power. Whenever you attempt something new, you'll feel fear. That type of fear doesn't mean stop; it means you are leaving your comfort zone. That's all. Every goal should scare you a little and excite you a lot. Ego will keep us safe; spirit will push our comfort zone a bit. The more spiritually developed among us will know that the "safe fear" of doing what you haven't done before is the way to go. It may give you a tingling, but that's not fear, that's excitement.

Should you be broke and struggling while reading this, it's time to look in the mirror and discover your beliefs. The meaning they give an event is the belief that attracted it. I'll repeat that: The meaning they give an event is the belief that attracted it. What does the current lack of funds mean? How do you tell your story about it? What you say reflects the beliefs causing it. Change the beliefs and you'll change the reality. As all spirituality teaches, change is an inside job.

In my Miracles Coaching® program, we guide people to explore their own limiting beliefs about money. At the core of my method is the knowing that spirituality is the power source of life. Everything else is an illusion. It all seems real. But the reality we perceive is an apparency. It's seen through our unconscious belief filters. It's our version of reality, not reality. Once we get back to the internal source of All That Is, and work from it, we can virtually have anything we can imagine, including money.

Light Practice

One meditation I teach that can help you know the spirituality of money, and empower you to accomplish what others might call impossible, goes like this:

Notice your thoughts. Even as you read these words, you are thinking. Words come and go, thoughts come and go, questions come and go. But notice you are not your thoughts. You are observing them. You are a witness to them. In short, you are not your thoughts but the viewer of them.

Now notice your emotions. How are you feeling? You may be happy, sad, curious, upbeat, confused, or anything else. But note that you have emotions, and are not your emotions. You are separate from them. You can describe them. You can observe them. You can witness them. Again, you are not your emotions but a reporter of them.

Now notice your body. You may have a few aches. You may need to adjust your seat. You may need to stretch. But notice you have a body, and are not your body. You can observe it, describe it, and be a witness to it. Once again, you are not your body but a spectator of it.

Finally, if you are not your thoughts, and you are not your

emotions, and you are not your body, who or what are you?

My answer is that you are the spiritual energy behind it all. You are The Witness of life. It's at this core observer level that you can have, do, or be what you can imagine, simply because at that level, there are no limits. You have the knowing that anything is possible, because spirit is unlimited.

Our work is to align with that spirit. As we do so, and as we drop limiting beliefs about life, we are free to use everything life offers to complete our life mission, including cash. Money isn't bad. Money is a symbol. Money is an energy. Money is a neutral and handy tool to accomplish your dreams and goals. The spiritual person has a knowing that whatever can assist them in manifesting their life calling is of the Light, and that includes money.

Money doesn't have any beliefs about you. You have beliefs about money. Once you know your beliefs are limiting your spiritual awakening, you are free to attract money, use money, appreciate money, and fulfill your Soul's purpose with money.

~Joe Vitale

About Joe Vitale

Dr. Joe Vitale—once homeless but now a motivating inspirator known to his millions of fans as "Mr. Fire!"—is the globally famous author of numerous bestselling books, such as *The Attractor Factor, Zero Limits, Life's Missing Instruction Manual, The Secret Prayer, The Awakened Millionaire,* and *Attract Money.*

He is a star in the blockbuster movie and book, *The Secret,* as well as a dozen other films. He has recorded many bestselling audio programs, from *The Missing Secret* to *The Zero Point.* He travels the world, from Russia and Poland to Peru and Kuwait, igniting the fire of inspiration within people. He's been on numerous domestic and international television shows, from Larry King Live to ABC, NBC, CBS, CNN, Fox and Friends, and more. He's also the world's first self-help singer-songwriter, with fifteen albums out and many of his songs nominated for the Posi Award (considered the Grammy's of positive music).

He created Miracles Coaching®, The Awakening Course, The Secret Mirror, Hypnotic Writing, the Awakened Millionaire Academy, and many more life transforming products and services. He lives outside of Austin, Texas with his wife, Nerissa, and their pets.

His main website is *www.MrFire.com*

Selfless Service

By Tammy Kling

If you can't get a miracle, be one.

~Nick Vujicic

What's your legacy? If you've discovered it, you know the peace and contentment that comes with that discovery, because it's like finding a magic treasure chest overflowing with diamonds and gold.

But if you have not, the opposite can be true. When you do not know what you're living for or why you're on this magnificent planet, each day is tainted by the feeling that there's something more. The lack of peace is like a shark prowling the ocean floor. You can't see it, but it's there, just beneath the surface.

Your legacy is your Light. It's the gift you will consciously share with the world. Before I knew what mine was, I recall sleepless nights and restless days that signified the transition to step into my life's calling. That season of discontent was brief, but it began as I stood in the middle of the Colombian jungle, as an airline crisis team leader. An airplane had crashed with hundreds on board, and I was thrust into the position of managing the unmanageable; the emotions of the families of the passengers who had been on that flight.

We searched for survivors, but there would not be more than a handful.

Hundreds of lives had been lost, and I was face-to-face with the parents, children, friends, and loved ones as it was all unfolding. Imagine being placed squarely in the center of a horror movie, only the movie never ends. That incident was a crossroads moment. It was an event that changed my life and the lives of others, forever.

Inner knowing

After that moment I had a deep knowing that selfless service was exactly what I wanted to spend my life doing. I needed my life's work to be fully committed to serving others, and I knew that I also wanted to inspire people to become world changers.

I traveled to Romania that same year and volunteered to work in an orphanage near Transylvania, in a town called Brasov. We flew over on the long and grueling flight with a team of volunteers, and when we arrived I played with orphans, helped at mealtimes, offered smiles and hugs, and helped transform the walls from a stark white, painting them with brightly colored animals. I am not an artist, but I did it, and I had a deep knowing inside that this was exactly where I was supposed to be.

Each day at the orphanage our team would arrive to help the staff distribute donations, and on some days the leader of the organization there would take us on excursions into town, yet I always felt a longing to be back with the children. This is the contagion that is the art of service. It gets into your blood and becomes a powerful addiction. Helping others helps yourself.

One specific night at two in the morning I laid awake in my bed, considering the idea to develop a foundation to build playgrounds in the yard of the orphanages, and most of all to engage the local community in our endeavors.

We figured that if we could teach them how to turn their hearts towards bringing Light into the orphan's lives, that we could make a difference even after we were gone.

Selfless service generates the power of multiplication

This is the primary principle of giving. It is not about you, nor might it even be about the one person you assist. Through the power of selfless service you ignite the power of multiplication.

The one life you pour into is restored. That individual is taught to mentor, give back, and pour into another life simply by your example. It is a domino effect that impacts generations. Save one life and you save a family. Save a family and you save the next generation.

If you have not yet discovered your greater purpose, chances are you've had seasons of angst, restlessness, or anxiety. We humans are mind, body, and Soul. We can strive and achieve and build and create and do. But if we do not fulfill that spiritual side of who we are, it feels as if something is missing.

At some point in life most people realize that there is more than just what we have worked for. We discover our gift of giving, and the powerfully regenerative process it creates.

Selfless service means giving back to others to create a better planet, a stronger world, and what I call legacy. When you give consciously, intentionally, and consistently, your heart is restored. It becomes interwoven with the heartbeat of humanity.

Legacy

Legacy is a five-hundred year plan. It is a specific intentionality about creating something that will live far beyond you.

Mother Teresa has a legacy that has lasted beyond her years. No matter what happens from this point on, nothing can take away the fact that her reputation and legacy is of selfless service to others. There are many other people in the world we could think of who have given of themselves to create transformation and change. But you do not have to be famous in order to do that. You can create change wherever you are, in your corner of the world, right now.

My friend, Nick Vujicic, was born with no arms or legs. Yet he has turned his adversity into his gift, and he speaks to audiences of hundreds of thousands of people, and has met with many world leaders. He is a spiritual teacher and motivational speaker. Nick often says, "If you can't get a miracle, be one."

Beautiful. And simple.

The key to living a life of abundance and contentment is to unlock your legacy, fulfill your life's destiny, and serve with a selfless heart.

Selfless service is the ability to give back to others, selflessly. What drives it? Can the desire to serve be created in someone who has never lived that way before? The answer is yes, most certainly, and I've seen even the hardest of hearts melt on the sidewalk beside me, as we looked into the eyes of a homeless man. When you ask others to give with you, you ignite change, and open their lives up to a concept that's so much bigger than themselves.

My story

When I worked in those orphanages in Romania, I fell in love with the orphan heart instantly, because I had one.

My own father had committed suicide when I was seven, and I always had a longing for him that felt like a gaping hole in my heart. Serving in Romanian orphanages was certainly a part of my healing process, which was a big aspect of sharing my Light.

When you give the gift of yourself and your words, you have the ability to change and save someone's Soul. Even your own. It stays with you, and when you look back even many years later, the memories bring new revelation.

On that first day in the orphanage I recall a significant moment when it occurred to me that the children had no identity.

I rremember walking through the cold hallways of the concrete building with the big surly, round headmistress, as she gave us a tour. The walls were a stark white. The room that the orphans slept in was lined with cribs, and even the older larger children were sleeping inside them, their arms and legs crunched up against the bars.

When we reached the community bathroom, I saw that there were no mirrors on the walls. I stopped for a moment, trying to figure it out. The sinks were there, but the mirrors had been ripped out. You could see the holes where the bolts had been. I asked the headmaster about this and the translator said that they were removed so that every orphan could be the same. So no one was different than the other.

In the bathroom with no mirrors, the children could not see their brilliant eyes, unique features, or mischievous smiles. It was impossible to tell them apart.

You could not discern between a boy and a girl. This broke my heart even more as I realized that their entire identity had been stripped away. Their shoes were the exact same color and style, tiny sneakers that had been donated. Their T-shirts and shorts were exactly the same. No dresses, no pinks, and no blues.

I picked up one child thinking it was a little boy, and the child hugged me and grabbed me, and it was actually a little girl. When I hugged and played with the orphans they would grasp my neck tightly and beg me not to leave. I regret today, even as I write this, that I didn't take one home. I wanted to. Oh how I wanted to. But that's a story for a different day.

Instead I went back again for years working in the orphanages. I bought lumber and built swing sets and shipped thousands of dollars of tools to Romania, so that the orphans could play.

Look inside your heart

My selfless service, or desire to help others, arose from a passion inside my heart to help the orphans see that they were as worthy as any child on the planet.

It is very likely that your own calling and the way that you give will be linked to a dormant passion in your heart. It doesn't have to be for orphans, but it will likely be rooted in a desire to give back because you see or feel a need.

I felt drawn to the orphans in Romania because when I

looked into their eyes I saw myself. I saw a child whose father did not love them enough to stay. I saw a child whose mother did not love him enough not to abandon them on the street, to leave them behind to become one of the voiceless children who may never have a home.

This entire experience impacted me so much that it crushed my heart. I recall going back to my flat at night unable to sleep, thinking of those orphans in their cribs. This is what empathy does for you. The problems of others become your problems. They are knitted into your Soul.

You can give up and give in, or use your anger and frustration to fuel a movement that will change the world.

I wanted to do something. I *had* to do something. At the time, Romania was a very divided society. The average salary was $50 a month, and when we gave a teenage girl we had taken under our wing a $20 bill, she screamed and told me to put my money away before a robber robbed us. When I began talking to a gypsy child on the sidewalk, the locals frowned and scolded us. That same teenage girl said, "Do not feed them, they are gypsies!" A gypsy was a different race then the typical Romanian. You did not intermingle. But to me, the seven-year-old on the street was the same as the seven-year-old in the orphanage. Or the seven-year-old in your house or mine.

If we are to change the world, we must see things from the bigger picture, outside of ourselves.

When I began writing, I wrote a book called *The Compass* and in it I said that "old pain is an anchor."

Indeed, it is true that you cannot carry old pain with you or it will become an anchor that ties you to the past, and prevents you from becoming all that you can be. It will infect your relationships like a cancer, and old triggers will set you off, creating disruption or fear or rejection and angry outbursts.

You must let go

Selfless service evolves from pain. You must use that old

event or tragedy or breakup or loss for the kindling of a majestic fire that transforms lives.

Once I realized how lost the city we were in was as a whole, and how detached people were from each other, I decided to do something about it.

The citizens were just survivors, fighting for their own families and life. When the teenage girl brought us home to her parents, they greeted us with hard-boiled eggs, and soda. She explained that this was a meal reserved just for us, and that's when the magnitude of their poverty set in.

When I went to the kitchen I noticed the cat dish had carrots and water in it because that was all they had. We spent the night in their home to be hospitable, and when it was time for a shower there was no water.

We decided to continue the mission to build playgrounds. We did not know why, and we did not know how, but we did it because we wanted to give back.

We went to the lumberyard and bought wood and bolts and we recruited locals and built playgrounds outside of the orphanages. We decided to gather our new friends, the Romanians, and teach them how to be givers.

We engaged them in the building of the swing sets, and we returned time and time again.

What is your legacy? Perhaps you're feeling a deep call, or a pull in a certain direction, but you don't yet know exactly how to proceed. Follow the Light, follow that knowing deep in your heart, and put one foot in front of the other.

You can solve a lot of the world's problems simply by solving one human issue in your neighborhood, family, or a town. You can create connectedness, giving, and a movement simply from a face-to-face encounter. It does not require a 12-step program, and it does not even require a massive social media campaign, or a GoFund me account.

Elie Wiesel is a concentration camp survivor who witnessed the murder of his family in the Nazi concentration camp in Germany. He said, "We are all connected by pain."

Selfless service originates from a pain or a passion in your heart. It comes from a feeling unlike any other. And guess what? It brings joy.

Giving back

When you are selfless, you have no desire to get anything in return.

Since those moments in Romania, that feeling of wanting to give back has never left me. Once you get a taste of it, it's like a powerful drug. The most powerful drug in the world is seeing someone who is hopeless given hope.

You can do many things in life, but if you do not give back of yourself to other human beings, your life will be devoid of meaning.

Selfless service is one of the highest spiritual teachings available, because you are multiplying others. Think about the ways you can start. What is it that you feel most passionate about? Where do you see the biggest injustice that causes pain in your heart?

You do not have to think too much about this. Make a decision today to be a world changer. World changers change the world.

When it was time for spring break last year, I loaded my children in the car with bags of clothing and cases of water and drove several hours to a town that had just been decimated by a tornado. When we pulled up, the entire town was flattened. The school, the hospital, the houses. It was unlike anything I ever expected to see.

The tornado had devastated entire streets of homes, and when my boy walked up to the rubble of a mansion, he leaned over and picked up a children's book in the front yard. He opened it, and as I watched him I wondered about the child that had been reading that book.

It was a moment to change their lives forever. Selfless service removes your ego, erases your problems, and transforms your life. It alters your reality immediately as you begin to see that you are not alone. That there are others who need much more.

Words are currency

Today I have a homeless organization that restores homeless lives and families with the power of words.

When I was asked to do a TEDx talk, I chose the topic of how to save a life, and I began by saying that, "Words are Currency."

When you begin to think this way, you realize that words are far more valuable than any dollar in your bank account. Words save lives, stop and start wars, prevent suicide, build nations and communities. Words truly are currency, and you can decide whether you want to be rich or poor depending upon how you use yours.

Today I have an amazing company built on the power of words, and my desire for selfless service. It's what I call a hybrid company, and we employ homeless writers. It isn't about giving them a job; it's about giving them a future. Imagine the power of living behind a dumpster and then being given a purpose in life.

They don't start as writers. They start by writing out their life story, by writing down their struggles and pain, and recovering in the process.

During this endeavor I have met and mentored many different homeless people. I have met them on streets and in shelters and under bridges, and brought them water and food and journals and words. Sometimes, I bring my kids. If we cannot teach our next generation to be the Light, what can we teach them?

During this process I met a homeless man named Dave, whose mind was sharp and whose body was old and frail. He was walking through a tent city, part of my volunteer team of doctors, specialists, and other selfless givers. Dave had jumped in the van to go along with us to help other homeless men, and we found a city nestled in a clump of trees on the outskirts of a major highway. Homeless men and women had gathered around a makeshift campfire for their morning coffee, and when we walked in through a thick covering of trees, there were various neighborhoods within the city that consisted of different cardboard "houses" on the left, and then another section farther back that had tents, and a house built from sticks and patchwork quilts. The house handcrafted of quilts reminded me of the forts I used to make as a kid, and I imagined the homeless resident that slept there lying awake at night, remembering those days.

These homeless cities are sub cities of sorts; cities within cities, hidden and self-contained. They exist all over the world, many buried deep into the heart of a real city with skyscrapers and restaurants and fancy theaters. The real cities are planned, architected, funded, and developed by city planning committees, degreed architects inside large firms, project managers, bankers, bonds, politicians, and city councils. They are built on solid ground, dirt that has been surveyed and tested and cleared. The sub cities are spur of the moment concoctions, built on desperation.

As I walked through the homeless city, I asked Dave questions about his life, and learned that he had an MBA, and had once had a family, a house on a cul-de-sac in a nice subdivision, and a prestigious career. I saw the lost potential in his eyes, and the defeat in his spirit. He was gruff and angry, answering my gentle questions as if he was tired of explaining his condition in life. We stood together while a physician examined a wound on a homeless man and changed a bandage. Another homeless man drank coffee from a dirty paper cup, and another sipped from a can of beer. After that day I knew I wanted to help Dave. My heart was filled with a longing to get him back on his feet, reconnected to his grown children, and beyond the shame and hopelessness of his situation. Like Legend, a little homeless boy who I brought home once to feed, nurture, and mentor, I felt a deep knowing that I could be the one thing in his life that could be a catalyst for hope.

The reason most people do not reach out to others, the reason that there's this unique category I refer to as "world changers" is because the rest do not know where to start.

Like anything new, they're locked up in indecision about how to proceed, or they've got preconceived notions and fears. Aren't you afraid you'll get harmed? People ask. "No," I reply. "I'm afraid they will."

If you can deliver Light to one human life in a simple conversation, you will see transformation. Just one conversation can turn things around.

I brought Dave to my home to help him write his resume and when he gave me his history I was so shocked I had to google him. Sure enough the image staring back at me was Dave, in his former role as a police chief! This old frail man living on the floor of the shelter for the past several years was once a decorated police chief in several major cities.

He had no addiction, he did not do drugs or alcohol, but like most of the homeless people I work with, he had a mortal wound. His was that his wife had divorced him and taken his two young kids. Along with that trauma he lost his job when he was replaced by a new police chief. Most people eventually recover but he could not handle the trauma. He went into a frozen state of depression that evolved into frustration and anger.

It took many weeks to get through to him and when I left him on that parking lot by the shelter and drove away he said to me sarcastically, "Oh yeah, don't worry, go back to your beautiful life. I'll just stay here, homeless."

I have to admit that his comment stayed with me. That night when I heard the rain on my roof, I thought of Dave. Where was he? Where was he sleeping? I worried about him.

I went back downtown, and I talked to him again. "Great news!" I said, "a CEO friend has offered to hire you at his company."

"What's the company?" he asked, and when I told him he scoffed. The company did not have a great reputation, and Dave didn't even want to attend the interview. "Look," he said, "I don't believe in that industry and I'm not going to compromise my principles." Dave held firm, and was still focused on getting something in law enforcement. "I want to be a police chief," he said.

I sat him down and looked him in the eye.

"Dave, you're a new creation; a wonderful, intelligent man. The past is gone and now you've got a blank canvas. You can be anything you want to be. I want you to start writing your story."

I knew if I could get him focused on that idea that he'd wake up each day with a purpose. He would write, he would heal, and in the process he would become a writer. And that's exactly what happened. The shelter got Dave a computer and set it up for him, and he developed a routine of writing every day. He sent me some of the most remarkable stories and I complimented and coached him and remained a constant source of encouragement. Words matter. For the first time in years, he had someone giving him words to empower.

Get out there and give. Be a world changer and change the world. Be the Light.

The meaning of life is giving. Selfless service is a legacy that leaves your imprint on the world.

~Tammy Kling

About Tammy Kling

Tammy Kling is a humanitarian and bestselling author. Her book, *The Compass*, has sold in several countries. Compared to the book the *Alchemist*, *The Compass* lesson, "old pain is an anchor" encourages you to let go. Tammy is the founder of the Homeless Writers and Speakers project restoring lives and families.

Her TEDx talk "How to save a life" is about the power of words. Tammy's focus is on communication that builds, elevates, and provides clarity. *Huffington Post* did a feature on Tammy called The Power of Words. Her work has been featured in the *New York Times*, *Wall Street Journal*, Dateline NBC, Extra, and Primetime.

Her book, *Words*, ignites people to understand that words are currency. Your story matters and your words are a legacy to change lives.

For more information, *www.tammykling.com*

Section 3

Sweating profusely, with sunburned skin and a limp, the traveler finally arrived at the lighthouse. He'd been expecting the grand structure to look extraordinary yet up close it appeared disappointingly ordinary.

He set his rucksack down and as he did so the lighthouse beacon ignited, and shone a vast column of Light onto him...not sunlight or artificial light. This was the Light of the Heavens.

Within the column of Light there flew a flutter of white butterflies, each radiating the same splendid Light as that of the column.

The traveler couldn't believe his eyes. He collapsed to the ground in sheer gratitude, in a state of utter surrender.

The Light

By John-Roger, D.S.S.

Wherever you find yourself, you can always choose or ask to have your best intentions revealed. The Light, among other good and wonderful things, does just that. This is all very simple. It can be easy if you will just let the Light radiate through your being and keep your intention on the Light for the highest good of all concerned.
~John Morton, D.S.S.

The Light is the energy of Spirit that pervades all levels of consciousness. It is an energy that is of God. It is pure, uncorrupted, and available for our use. Spirit is energy, the force that activates the human consciousness and gives it life. Spirit individualizes itself as Soul and so resides closely within each consciousness. Many people have said that a human being has a Soul, but it is closer to reality to say that the Soul has a human being.

The experience of God, with which we are all involved, is made up of positive energies and negative energies, much like a battery is made up of positive and negative energies. It takes both to make it a working unit. Present as the negative pole of this total spiritual experience are what we call the lower realms: the physical, astral, causal, mental, and etheric realms. Present as the positive pole are the Soul and Spirit as the pure energy of God. These two poles working together are what we call the Light.

The energies of the negative pole of experience are more apparent when you are here in the physical realm. This level is their territory and they can be quite powerful. But as you attune your consciousness more and more to the energies of the positive pole, to your spiritual self, you find that the spiritual Light can override any negativity. You learn to bring all the levels of your consciousness into the flow of the Light; then the positive energy extends itself through all the negative realms, and you find every level of your life becoming a manifestation of God's love and grace.

The energy of the Light is the spiritual force that is present within and that activates all things. It is everywhere to a greater or lesser degree. The Light is more active in a tree than it is in a rock, and it is more active in a deer than it is in a tree, but it is present in all of them, although they may not be consciously aware of it. The presence of the Light is most active within the human consciousness, and the human consciousness is unique in its ability to be consciously aware of the Light and to work as a co-creator with the energy of Light.

The magnetic Light and the spiritual Light

There are two aspects of the energy of the Light. One is magnetic in nature and is an energy of the lower realms (up through the etheric realm). You, consciously or unconsciously, are an individual director of it. When you work with this Light for your highest good and for the highest good of everyone, you may also activate the spiritual Light, which comes from the positive realms of pure Spirit (the Soul realm and above). When you activate this higher Light (also called the Light of the Holy Spirit), you can experience at-one-ment with God, and the results in your life and in the lives of those around you can be quite wonderful. In the lower realms, you cannot get the Holy Spirit without the magnetic Light because the Holy Spirit rides on the magnetic Light, but you can get the magnetic Light without the Holy Spirit. It takes a greater attunement to get the Holy Spirit.

This higher Light (the Holy Spirit) will never inflict itself on anyone or anything and comes only when invited. It can be active only when you are consciously pure in your intent and expression. You are pure in your expression when you ask for the Light to be present for the highest good. You do not condition the Light by asking it to do what you feel would be right or what you think would be right. When you just ask for the presence of the Light and ask Spirit to bring forward whatever is for the highest good, that is when you are Light: Living In God's Holy Thoughts.

The magnetic Light is neither good nor bad; it depends on how it is used. It can be used, along with the spiritual Light, for those things that are positive and that enhance the spiritual evolution of each consciousness. The magnetic Light can also be used in negative ways. It is the energy field that people tap into when they use the force of their consciousness to control another person or to bring harm or hurt to another. Spiritual law says that all creations are returned to the creator, so it follows that any harm or hurt you perpetrate will be returned to you (see my chapter, Karma and Destiny, in *The Light: A Book of Wisdom*).

Just as everyone is an extension of God, through individualized Soul, so is everyone the Light. All people have this energy of Light present with them to various degrees, and all possess various abilities to express it and work with it. Some people are more attuned to the magnetic Light, and some are more attuned to the spiritual Light. Wherever you find yourself is fine. All the levels are steps along the way of your spiritual evolution.

You do it yourself

One religious concept that has been prevalent throughout history is that the priest, minister, or guru is somehow special and has a greater attunement to the spiritual Light. Thus, many people look to a "special one" as the savior or the intermediary with God. In the last few decades, a whole new consciousness has been moving across the planet, saying that each person is special, and that as each develops their inner spiritual awareness, each has the ability to become attuned to the spiritual Light through their own consciousness. So each person starts their own salvation. Each person becomes the teacher, the student, the worker, and the harvester of their own beingness.

Too often, however, people want to yoke themselves to someone outside of themselves in the physical world and say, "Do it for me." This will probably not work and will usually delay your spiritual unfoldment. This does not mean you do it all by yourself. No way. We are all connected, we are all dependent upon one another to some extent, and no one is going to do everything by himself or herself. You may want a wayshower, a guide, someone to point the direction, but do not let anyone do it for you. I do not do it for you. I show you techniques, methods, and ways. I tell you what has worked for me and what I know has worked for other people. But it could all appear to be a lie until you do it and it works for you. This is why I always advise people to "check it out" and get their own experience.

The position of the human consciousness is unique. God has given the human consciousness the ability to be aware of itself and to know God consciously. God has allowed us the position of co-creators and thereby given us the opportunity to learn responsibility to the Light within us. God has given us these beautiful realms of physical, emotional, mental, and unconscious existence and has supplied the magnetic Light of these levels to give us infinite opportunity to create. We can create many things, and God has instituted the law of karma so that we will always be made aware of our creations. It is feedback so we will know how we are doing.

Sharing your Light

As the human consciousness moves away from the negative creations of the magnetic Light towards the positive creations of the spiritual Light, it comes closer and closer to God and the Soul; that individualized spark of God within. Some people let that Light shine through their expression more readily than others, and these are the ones who are happy, smiling, and nice to be around; the ones who can lift you just by being there.

When you come from that center of Light, you expand your ability to love and to share with people, to reach out and touch them. You expand your ability to say in many ways, "Thank you for being here." Maybe you think you could not say that to anyone, that it would sound namby-pamby, but why ignore others when they really need a pat on the back and a verification that they are doing okay? Sometimes it is in the smallest areas that people need your Light and Love the most. Sometimes that pat on the back and a quick, "It's really nice to see you" can do so much to awaken the consciousness of Light in others. They can suddenly stand up and face the day. That service of love may be returned to you at a later time and it is nice to reap those rewards.

Many years ago I knew the principal of a high school who did not let his Light shine through very much. He would walk through the halls really down in the mouth, and he seldom smiled. Every time he was around, he created a lot of tension, and the teachers and students would think, "I wonder what's wrong? I wonder if I've done something wrong?" After a couple of years, he was transferred to another school, and the new principal would smile, laugh, and share his beingness with the faculty and students. When he liked something, he would say so, and when he didn't he would suggest changes. It was amazing how the morale of the entire school lifted because one man let the Light within him shine out and expressed the love he felt for the people around him.

Working with the Light

Wherever you go, ask for God's Light to surround you, protect you, and fill you for the highest good. Place it ahead of you wherever you are going so that you will always be well-received. And each time you meet someone, ask that this Light be placed between the two of you, not as a barrier, but as that which can clarify. If you do that, everything that comes to you will come through the Light.

Learning to let the spiritual Light flow can be one of your

most rewarding experiences. That Light within you will guide you as you learn to attune yourself to its direction. If you get in your car and ask for the Light to surround and protect you and then you speed, the Light is probably not going to do a whole lot for you. It may be that the "white Light" you called in to help you asks the "red light" for a special assist. But if you get in the car and attune yourself to the Light within you, you are probably going to drive to the speed limit, be careful, and watch. Then it is very easy for the Light to work with you.

When you work with the Light, you walk within the most absolute protection that exists. It is so perfect and so absolute that you may not even know you are being guided out of areas potentially disastrous for you. Perhaps you get tied up in traffic or delayed in some other way and later find out that, had you been on time, you might have been involved in a tremendous wreck. You have heard stories of people missing a plane for all sorts of strange reasons, and that plane crashes, killing all aboard. This may be the Light in action. When you get delayed or caught up on some unexpected happenstance, you may never be aware when it is the means to protect you from disaster. So do not be too quick to judge your experience. What you see as an irritation may be your greatest protection, the greater manifestation of Spirit working in your life.

You might think that if you use the Light as protection, you should be able to walk down a dark alley in the middle of the night, safe from all harm. But if the Light is really working for you in the highest way, it might not have you walking down a dark alley in the middle of the night in the first place. Instead, you will be somewhere else, safe from harm. Using the Light does not mean that you can be irresponsible in your actions. If you are open to the Light, develop your awareness of it, and learn to flow with it, you can find your life unfolding in the most beautiful, dynamic, creative, and loving ways imaginable.

You know, hindsight is twenty-twenty vision. You say, "I shouldn't have done that. I should have done this other thing." In retrospect, you know what would have been the right action, the Light action. Foresight is wisdom, given to the few who will look forward. But "heresight" is available to all who will use it. If you are living here and watching, you will not need hindsight because there will be no regrets, and you will have no concern for the future because when you are living here, you are adaptive and can handle whatever comes to you.

You can always handle the present moment; there is never any difficulty in that. The difficulty comes when you allow your mind and your emotions to split off into yesterday or tomorrow and dissipate your energies. That is what happens; the energies split and you think, "I'm really falling apart. I have to get more rest. I'd better get to bed." So you go to bed, and the Soul can then leave the body and go into an energy field of pure Light and regain the quiet contentment of pure beingness. The mind and emotions quiet down. Then the Soul comes back and recharges the body with positive, spiritual Light and you wake up in the morning feeling much better. You say, "I really feel together today," and you are. The energies are all together and present in the here and now.

Light columns

We have a guideline in the Movement of Spiritual Inner Awareness (MSIA), which is to always leave something better than you found it. One way I do this is to plant Light columns everywhere I go. For example, many years ago when I was in Mexico, I climbed to the top of the Pyramid of the Sun and placed a Light column there. I returned a few years later and could see the Light column from miles away. I could see it as a big, shimmering, white-purple haze in the air above the pyramid. It had held solidly, and that was so nice because a lot of people got into the spiritual Light frequency as they climbed to the top of the pyramid.

This is how you can place a Light column: for the highest good, envision or intend a funnel or pillar of Light from the highest place you can imagine going right through you and into the very core of the earth. That is all you need to do. The Light column you place may be effective for two days, thirty minutes, or fifteen years. Its duration does not matter, and you do not even need to concern yourself with that since Spirit is actually doing it. Perhaps a Light column will hold for two hours, which may be the exact amount of time it was needed in that area.

If you are in one area day after day, continue to place Light columns there. People who have used this technique in their homes and offices have noticed positive results. It is a beautiful and effective way to clean up your immediate environment. You can also do this throughout the city you live in. For example, it used to be that you could go up and down New York City and only see shadows, but now you can see a lot of Light there. I flew over New York City once and thought there was smog over the city, but when I looked again, I realized, "Good gravy! That whole city has a haze of white Light all over it." I sat back in the seat, tears came to my eyes, and I thought, "Somebody in New York, at least one person, knows how to do this." I found out later that the MSIA ministers in New York had been all up and down Manhattan Island, in the subways and everywhere, placing columns of Light.

A lady from New York said to me, "Have you noticed in the last few years that New York's vibration has lifted? It's lighter, it's nicer, it's better." I definitely agreed and told her, "I don't feel the negativity in my stomach and across my back. I'm looking forward to coming here more often."

Placing Light columns is a way to integrate into your daily life and routine a specific awareness of Spirit. When you do this, you are using your spiritual energy in positive action that can bring positive results to the physical level. It is wonderful when more and more people are willing to say, "I'm a Light bearer. I'll bear Light wherever I go." As a spiritual being, you have inside the ability to call forth and bring forth the Light of God into any environmental situation and to transmute the negativity into a positive gain. As one example of this, to help stabilize the earth, you can ask that a column of Light be placed into the center of the Earth and then radiate to the north and south poles. This can help areas that are prone to earthquakes.

Light columns can be as big as a drinking glass, as thin as a pencil, as large as a house, as huge as an entire city, or like the Washington Monument. Have you ever seen the sun shining through a window and seen dust particles floating in the air? A Light column will sometimes look very much like that. When you see that kind of Light energy or force, you may think your vision is a little disturbed, but it may be that you are tuning in to higher frequencies and seeing a little more than the physical realm. That is good news. Of course, you might not visually perceive the Light columns, and you certainly do not have to. Not seeing them does not in any way lessen your ability to create them. You will probably never know directly the benefit that such work has, the ways it touches to people, or the positive changes it brings about. It is a silent work, a silent ministry, and a powerful one.

The Light is the energy of Spirit that pervades all levels of consciousness. It is an energy that is of God. It is pure, uncorrupted, and available for our use.
~John-Roger, D.S.S

About John-Roger

A teacher and lecturer of international stature, John-Roger is an inspiration in the lives of many people around the world helping people to discover the Spirit within themselves and find health, peace, and prosperity.

With two co-authored books on the *New York Times* bestseller list and more than four dozen self-help books and audio albums, John-Roger offers extraordinary insights on a wide range of topics. He is the founder of many organizations, including the nondenominational Church of the Movement of Spiritual Inner Awareness (MSIA), the University of Santa Monica; Peace Theological Seminary & College of Philosophy; the Institute for Individual and World Peace,and The Heartfelt Foundation.

John-Roger has given over six-thousand lectures and seminars worldwide, many of which are televised nationally on his cable program, That Which Is, through the Network of Wisdoms. He also co-wrote and co-produced the movies Spiritual Warriors and The Wayshower.

To learn more about the information presented in this chapter, please refer to John-Roger's book *Fulfilling Your Spiritual Promise*. John-Roger passed away on October 22 2014. His work continues on.

For more information, visit *www.john-roger.org*

Stepping into the Light

By Anita Moorjani

If Light is in your heart, you will find your way home.
~**Rumi**

I was diagnosed with lymphoma in 2002, which is cancer of the lymph glands. In the space of four years, it spread throughout my entire lymphatic system, and the top half of my torso was covered with tumors, some the size of lemons.

When I had cancer I was extremely fearful of everything. Not only was I afraid of the cancer itself, growing within my body, but also that all of my actions were feeding the cancer. So I spent most of my time researching the cancer, doing everything I could to fight it and get rid of it. I tried every kind of healing modality possible. In addition, I took many different nutritional supplements, and read a huge amount of information, all of which conflicted with each other. One day I'd read that doing a particular thing was good for me, and then another day I'd read elsewhere that it was, in fact, bad for me. Therefore, I constantly lived in fear. I was afraid of the foods I was eating. I was afraid of using plastic. I was afraid of using microwaves. I was afraid of eating sugar. I was afraid that if I ate too many carbohydrates it would turn into sugar and feed the cancer cells...and so on. As you can imagine, life wasn't much fun!

As time progressed my body continued to deteriorate. Every day I'd wake up and think, "Oh God, I've got to fight this cancer for another day." Almost four years later, my body had completely wasted away. I weighed about 85 pounds and I looked like a skeleton. I couldn't walk because my muscles had wasted away, and I spent my time either in a wheelchair or sitting up in an armchair. The large open skin lesions covering my torso were weeping with toxins. My lungs were filled with fluid, so if I lay down for too long I'd choke, and I was constantly connected to a portable oxygen tank. I lived like that for at least six months—and my health deteriorated rapidly over that period of time. The doctors told my husband that I only had three months to live at the most. At this point I was still living at home, cared for by a nurse. The doctors didn't tell me I was going to die, but I guessed that was the case. I felt absolutely petrified of dying. I believed in karma and reincarnation, but I still carried a great fear of death, and I didn't want to leave Earth.

Expanded consciousness

My main thought at that time was, 'How am I going to get out of this?' I constantly asked, 'What do I need to do to get out of this? What shall I research? What have I missed? What shall I read next? What have I got wrong? Who do I need to talk to?' I wanted to leave no stone unturned. Finally, on the night of Feb 1, I surrendered. I slipped into a coma and I was taken to the hospital. The doctors told my husband that my organs had shut down and that the dying process had begun. They said, "She's not going to come out of the coma." Yet the remarkable thing was, that while in the coma I could see, hear, and feel everything going on around me. I could hear the doctor's words, and I could see and feel my husband and mother, who were distraught.

Time is not linear in that realm so it felt like all of time was happening at once. I was aware of everything happening around me, and I felt incredibly light and free. I was pure awareness, as my body was separate from me. All that pain, suffering, and discomfort from the body was gone. I was surrounded by a feeling of unconditional love; a kind of love that I'd never felt before. It was the most amazing feeling of love ever. I felt like I was loved just because I existed and I didn't need to do everything to prove myself. Even when I became aware of my grieving family, I felt assured that they'd be okay. I didn't feel that I'd miss them as I didn't feel separate from them. The body is what keeps us separate, but I felt I could be with them always, even in that state. I sensed that time was different, so they would join me in soon, even if that meant 20 years in Earth time. It felt like my consciousness had expanded so I was no longer looking with physical eyes. It felt like I was something much greater. I expanded beyond the room I was in, beyond the hospital, beyond the country. I became aware of everything. It was like I had 360-degree peripheral vision. Whatever I put my focus on, I was there. It was hard to believe that small insignificant body was me, because in this state I felt so powerful and strong.

In that moment, I realized that we are all Love at our core. Once we remove the physical body, our race, culture, gender, and beliefs, all that's left is our pure essence—our Soul—and that is pure God or Love. God isn't a physical being that is separate from any of us. In that state there's no separation. We all merge, we're all one, and we all share the same consciousness. There is no entity separate from you. You are everywhere, just as I am everywhere. Right now, here on Earth, we believe in separation because we think the physical body is all there is, but we are much more than our physical body. When we die we merge with God, so we have the same clarity and understanding God has. It feels like waking up from a dream. If you're having a terrible nightmare and you wake up with the clarity, 'Oh, it was a dream, this is what it's really like,' when we die, it feels the same and we say, 'Oh, this is what it really feels like!'

I didn't go through a tunnel of Light like some people who have a Near Death Experience (NDE) speak of, because my death wasn't sudden, such as a road accident or a heart attack; it was a gradual decline. I felt like I could be anywhere at any time. Time and space were no longer an obstacle. I even found myself with my brother, who was in India rushing to get to

Hong Kong before I died. Moving deeper into this realm, I became aware of people who had died before me; my father who had died ten years ago, and my best friend who had died two years prior to that. I became aware that I was surrounded by loving beings, but I didn't recognize them. I knew they were there to greet me, comfort me, and help me through the transition.

Living in fear

At one point I suddenly whooshed back into my body. I'd reached a point where I realized I could choose whether to stay on the other side or return into my body. My father said I couldn't go any further and that if I did, I couldn't turn back. He said, "It's not your time and you should go back into your body." However, I didn't want to go back as my body was still sick. I felt amazing where I was and I didn't want to leave. I knew that returning into a sick body would be a burden on both me and my family. But then, almost instantaneously, I understood the Truth of who I really am. I understood why I'd got the cancer in the first place. I was a people pleaser and I'd spent a lifetime beating myself up, making myself small, treating myself like a doormat, and I had never loved and valued myself. I had feared so many things, such as failing, upsetting other people, and even cancer itself. Every decision I had made in my life up until that that point had been driven by fear; a fear of not being accepted, and a fear of wanting to be liked. I did things out of fear, not out of love and passion. When I understood that, I knew life wasn't supposed to be hard. I was supposed to live a life of joy, and I instantaneously realized I was a powerful, magnificent being. I had never known that before. And the cancer was my body's way of communicating to me. It wasn't a punishment or my karma as I had previously believed; it was my own powerful energy that had turned inward, instead of expressing itself outwards in the powerful way it was supposed to. I then knew that if I chose to return to my body, the cancer would heal very quickly.

And as I knew wholeheartedly, within five weeks my cancer had indeed healed. The doctors were completely baffled, and they didn't know what to make of the news. Since then, many oncologists have researched my case, and I've appeared on TV several times, and on documentaries where my medical records were checked. To them, there was no logical explanation as to how my advanced cancer had healed so quickly. One oncologist said, whichever way he looks at it, I should be dead. Others said there are no records of anyone else who has come back from such a late stage of cancer and made such a full recovery at a rapid rate.

Being in that realm taught me that I'm not meant to live life from fear, so today I make decisions from a place of Love. Living from fear is the only way we, as a society, know. People think they have to teach their children to fear as that keeps them safe. But it doesn't. Love keeps you safe. If you love and value yourself, you won't put yourself in danger. Fear only immobilizes you.

Creating Heaven on Earth

I feel that we're meant to create the state of Love I felt in that other realm, right here. We're meant to create Heaven on Earth. I was delighted to have been given the chance to create Heaven on Earth, and all I wanted to do was talk about it and help people. But it transpired to be very frustrating for me because we live in a culture that doesn't support that way of being. We've created a society where everybody is hurting, everybody is in pain, everybody is stuck in this conditioning, trapped in the roles they've been doing for decades. And if they try to do some of the things they think will lead them to happiness, it means turning against what they've been taught. So I've found it very challenging and at times I've thought, 'Gosh, why did I even come back?' We were all born with this ability to tap into the Universal consciousness, but as children we are taught and conditioned not to trust it, and to live from our head not our heart. We are conditioned to believe that our physical body is all we have, and not to trust or believe anything that cannot be felt, heard or seen with our five senses. It's unfortunate, as it's like we have had our wings clipped. It's not necessary to go out and find the Universal consciousness and ocean of wisdom that I speak of. It's already within you. All you have to undo the layers of conditioning in order to get to it.

Knowing

We are all spiritual beings, whether we realize it or not. I used to think we had to work at being spiritual and so I was into meditation, prayer, and worshiping religious figures. But now I understand that it doesn't make a difference whether we believe in a religion or not—whether we believe in Jesus, Allah, Buddha, Shiva, none of them, all of them, or one of them. I now understand that these were prophets who lived at one time and all had similar messages, but they are all part of the same consciousness as you and I. It makes no difference who greets you in the other realm—it could be Jesus, Allah, Buddha, or your own grandmother; we all have access to the same knowledge. And when we cross over we immediately have access to that very same knowledge. When we lose the need to be greeted by a religious deity, then we clearly see what the Truth is. We are all connected and we all have access to the same power. Everybody has access to the power that healed me so rapidly. In most cases we block it by thinking we need to go to someone to heal us, and as a result we give our power away. But we don't have to do anything; it's enough to simply know it. Knowing is very different from believing or having faith in something…knowing means *really knowing*. For example, when I came out of the coma, my body was still covered in open skin lesions, I still weighed 85 pounds, and I was still hooked up to various machines and tubes. But I came out of the coma and told everybody I was going to be okay. I knew I was already healed and only my body had to catch up. It wasn't a feeling of, 'I'm going to be healed,' or trying to convince myself. I *knew*.

Life after the NDE

My life has changed dramatically since my NDE. I couldn't go back to work after my healing, as I had a completely different view of the world, and as a result, I became a bit of a loner. I lost a lot of my old friends as I no longer saw the world in the same way. I didn't have the same ambitions, such as making money and moving up the career ladder, or socializing and going out drinking. My new friends are very different than my old friends, but I'm much closer to them because they like me for who I really am. The life I was living before wasn't real—it was me constantly trying to be something, and doing what I felt was expected of me.

I began to share my story on the internet in the hopes that it would help people. Before long, it went viral and was discovered by the best-selling author, Dr. Wayne Dyer. He contacted his publisher, Hay House, and told them to read my story. Hay House emailed me asking if I'd like to publish a book of my story. I answered with, "Absolutely, I'd love that."

After the NDE I knew I didn't have to work at everything anymore. I simply needed to be myself, love myself, know that I'm worthy and deserving, and allow everything to unfold. The more we chase and pursue something, the more we send ourselves the message that it's elusive, that we don't deserve it, that we're not worthy of it, and that's why we have to work so hard to get it. The more you realize that you deserve it, and that you're worthy, the easier it is. It will fall into your lap much easier that way because you're not pushing it away with an energy of, "Oh my God, that's so out of reach. I've got to work really hard to chase it and beat out the competition." As soon as you know you're worthy of it, you will get it.

Unleashing the wisdom

After my journey, it took a few years for me to unravel all the new wisdom that I'd acquired—it all streamed out as I wrote my book, *Dying To Be Me*. This wisdom would have taken years to learn, but I learned it all while I was in a coma for 30 hours. That incredible experience changed me as a person. I learned that we live in a world that is completely upside-down, and teaches us all the wrong things—that's why everyone's getting sick, everyone's struggling, and relationships are failing. The answers are so simple but as humans we make life very complicated. Perhaps most prominently, I learned that love is the most important thing, which starts with learning to love and value our Self. Until we do that nothing else in our life will go right.

Conclusion: you are powerful

Everyone is valuable and powerful beyond anything they are capable of imagining. My advice is to let go of anyone who you perceive as a negative influence in your life, and know that it's not about you, it's about them. Life is a gift, so don't waste it. Learn to value yourself and your life, and live every day as though it's a gift and that you matter and you have a purpose. Find out who you are, and be who you are, express yourself, and shine your Light as brightly as you can. If you don't express yourself and be yourself fully then you're depriving the world of who you came here to be.

Light Practice

For those who are ill...don't obsess over your illness. In between your treatments continue to live a full life, find your joy, learn to love and value yourself. Ask yourself, 'What would I do if I could do anything at all? What would bring me the most joy?' And then do it. Learn to laugh every day, and don't obsess about your illness. See the treatments as running an errand, and don't revolve your life around them.

For those who are depressed...go on an inward journey to find out who you are. Even if you feel like you don't know your purpose, it's not about finding something to do, it's about finding out who you are, and then being and expressing that. Start by finding something that's fun and joyful. Ask yourself,

"What will make me happy? What will bring me happiness and joy?" Those are the clues to who you are and your purpose. Doing things that make you happy are the things that come most naturally to you.

For those who have lost a loved one...I believe death should be celebrated, but of course when we lose someone we love we're clearly going to miss them. Take time to grieve, but grieve for yourself, not for the dead person. The person (Soul) who has passed on is doing great, and they only want you to be happy. You needn't worry about doing the right ritual to ensure they reach the right place. Instead, do whatever you need to do to get to a place where you can find your joy again. There's no 'should.' Don't feel obligated to do something just because the church or temple says to.

For those looking for your purpose in life...it's not necessary to actively seek your life purpose. Allow yourself to who you are. Be authentic. Ask, "What makes me feel passionate? What brings me joy?" These are clues to finding out who you are. As you allow yourself to be who you are, your purpose will magically unfold before you.

You are a magnificent being of Light and you are here in this world to shine to your full potential.
~Anita Moorjani

About Anita Moorjani

Anita Moorjani has become something of an international sensation since her book, *Dying to be Me*, hit the *New York Times* bestsellers list only two weeks after its release in March, 2012. She had experienced what most people never have; she "crossed over," and came back to share what she learned. Her remarkable NDE and subsequent healing from end-stage cancer, is one of the most amazing cases ever recorded.

Born in Singapore of Indian parents, Anita is multi-lingual. She had been working in the corporate field for several years before her cancer diagnosis in 2002.

World-renowned author, Dr. Wayne Dyer was instrumental in bringing Anita's story to public attention, and wrote the foreword to her book. He subsequently invited her to appear on his TV special, "Wishes Fulfilled," which airs frequently on PBS.

Following the global success of her book, which is being translated and published into 36 languages, Anita has regularly been interviewed on various prime time television shows around the world, including "Fox News" in New York, and "The Jeff Probst Show" in Hollywood.

She inspires her audience to transform their lives by living more authentically, discovering their greatest passions, transcending their deepest fears, and living from a place of pure joy. Anita is currently one of the most sought after inspirational speakers in the world and addresses sell out audiences all over the globe.

For more information, *www.anitamoorjani.com*

Creating Heaven
on Earth

By Bruce Lipton

*There is no subject more crucial to our happiness and our
ability to live and give at our highest capacity.*
~Dr. Wayne Dyer

The biggest misunderstanding we humans have revolves
around our belief systems and who's running our life. We
must begin to recognize that we've been programmed, and
if we get out of the program then we will have the ability to
create a vastly different experience on this planet.

The background

About 47 years ago, before the world was aware of them,
I was cloning stem cells. A stem cell is the equivalent of an
embryotic cell in our body after we're born. Every day we lose
hundreds of billions of our cells through normal aging, and if
these cells aren't replaced then we'd die. The stem cells' function
is to divide and replace the lost cells, keeping us alive.

If I put one stem cell into a Petri-dish by itself, it divides
every ten hours, so at the end of a week I'd have about 50,000
cells in the Petri-dish, all genetically identical as they came
from the same single parent cell. If I take those cells and
split them into three different Petri-dishes, and I change the
environment (or culture medium) in each, I'd have three dishes
with genetically identical cells in each dish, but each with a
slightly different culture medium. In one dish the cells formed
muscle, in the second dish the cells formed bone, and in the

third dish the cells formed fat cells. So what controls the fate of the cells? The general belief is that genes control the cells, but they were all genetically identical—the only difference was in the chemistry of the environment. Therefore, the cells adjust their genetics according to their interaction with the environment.

The human body is made up of 50 trillion cells inside a skin covered body, which is like a skin covered Petri-dish with a culture medium called blood. The chemical composition of the culture medium determines the fate of the cells, and this is important because whether the cell is in a skin covered dish or a Petri-dish its fate is controlled by the environment, which is the medium: either blood in the body, or made-to-match blood in the Petri-dish. In the body the chemistry of the blood controls the state of the cells, and the brain controls the chemistry of the blood. The brain adds hormones, emotional chemicals, and growth factors to the blood, and this information is then used by the cells to control their behavior. The brain releases chemistry based on our perception or response to the environment. The mind records environmental information through all our receptors and then sends chemistry that matches our perception of the environment, which complements the environment of the cells. For example, if you see someone you love, the brain, in a perception of love, releases chemistry such as dopamine, which is experienced as pleasure, and a growth hormone that enhances the vitality of the cells. If we take the same chemicals released by a mind in love and put them into a plastic Petri-dish with cells, they grow beautifully. However, if that same person sees something that scares them, their mind will release stress hormones and inflammatory agents. If added to a dish with cells, fear chemicals cause the cells to shut down and die. Basically, the cells in our body are like cells in a Petri-dish, and the fate of the cells is controlled by the chemical composition of the growth medium. The chemistry that the brain releases is a reflection of how we perceive the world, which is the infamous mind-body connection. To conclude, in simple terms, the scientific studies reveal that our beliefs control our biology…not our genes as previously believed.

Falling in Love

In my seminars I ask people to remember a time when they fell in love, and then I ask two questions. Were you healthy? Most people say they were exuberantly healthy. And was life so beautiful that you couldn't wait to have more of that experience? Most people say, "Of course." When we fall in love our world changes, and we experience the equivalent of Heaven on Earth. People tend to think it was a coincidence that their life went so well after falling in love. But it was no coincidence. It involves understanding how our biology is connected to our perceptions, beliefs, and experiences. When we fall in love, we don't change our world. We change who we are. Then at some point that feeling fades and life becomes normal again. We create the Heaven on Earth experience with our conscious mind and lose it when the subconscious kicks in and plays disempowering, limiting, self-sabotaging programs from our child development years. By understanding this we can intervene, change the programming, and create Heaven on Earth throughout our entire life.

The conscious mind and the subconscious mind

The mind runs the biology in our life and controls our nervous system and our behavior. There are two parts to the mind: the conscious mind and the subconscious mind. Our creative conscious mind is connected to our personal identity, which is essentially who we are, and the source of our wishes, dreams, and desires. The subconscious mind, on the other hand, is similar to a record play back device. It records our life experiences and if we ever encounter those experiences again, it's not necessary to relearn our behavior in dealing with those experiences. Instead, we simply push the play button, and the subconscious automatically responds to those experiences. It's a million times more powerful than the conscious mind as it can control our whole life. From the third trimester of pregnancy to the first seven years of life, a child's brain primarily operates at the EEG theta brain state, a state of consciousness associated with imagination. However theta is also the state of mind for hypnosis. From this place, our minds are constantly recording the behavior of others (parents, family community). These downloaded behaviors represent the foundational rules of becoming a member of a family, a community, and a society. During this time, thousands of facts, rules, and behaviors are downloaded as programs in our brain. Psychologists recognize that the vast majority of these programs are disempowering, limiting, and self-sabotaging.

The conscious mind is not time-bound, so when someone asks, "What are you doing this week?" or, "What did you do last week?" the conscious mind disconnects from the current moment to review our memory. Each time the conscious mind isn't paying attention to the current moment, by default, behavior is switched to control by the subconscious programs. If our mind wanders, we play behaviors from programs we downloaded from others in the first seven years. When the conscious mind is busy and we kick into the default programs of the subconscious, we are not conscious of the behaviors we are expressing. Science has discovered that our conscious mind is busy in thought 95 percent of the time, meaning we're only directly controlling our lives with our true wishes and desires about 5 percent of the time. The rest of the time we're playing programs that we acquired from others before the age of seven.

Reprogramming the subconscious mind

So the question is, what would happen if we didn't default to the subconscious mind, but instead we ran our life from our creative conscious mind, which is in alignment with our wishes and desires? That's precisely what happens when we're in love. Scientists recognize that when we're in deep love, our conscious mind doesn't wander. Nevertheless, over time that loving feeling fades because life becomes busy, and we still have to pay the rent, fix the car, do the chores, and so on. As our conscious mind starts thinking about these tasks, by definition our mind isn't paying attention and we shift into the default programs of the subconscious mind. These programs do not necessarily support our wishes and desires at all. As a matter of fact, the majority of these unconscious behaviors usually conflict with that. As we play more and more of our subconscious programs, we start introducing a whole range of behaviors that weren't present when we first experienced love. And all of a sudden our relationship is no longer the juicy Heaven on Earth experience it was when we first fell in love. Now it's just like everyday life, and all that excitement and joy starts to dissipate. The simple conclusion is this: the Heaven on Earth experience is created when two people operate from their conscious mind, manifesting their wishes and desires. The Heaven on Earth experience ends when two uninvited minds—the subconscious minds—kick in with their programs, which are primarily disempowering, and the experience is diluted with negative behaviors. If we stay conscious we'll experience the Heaven on Earth feeling forever. Consider what would happen if we reprogram the subconscious mind, eliminating negative programs, and replacing them with the positive intentions from our conscious mind. When our minds wander and we default to subconscious control, we now would play all positive and supporting programs. The result is whether we are paying attention or not, we're still creating Heaven on Earth. By understanding the nature of how the conscious and subconscious minds interact, we can reprogram the subconscious mind and be free to create a life where Heaven on Earth becomes a part of everyday life.

When we keep our conscious mind in the present moment, whether it's because there's someone else bringing that Heaven on Earth experience into our life, or because of something we love to do, every decision and action we make is based on our wishes and desires rather than from disempowering automatic programs others have downloaded into our subconscious minds.

Psychologists suggest that 70 percent or more of behaviors downloaded into the subconscious during our developmental years are negative, so every time we flip into the subconscious we're likely engaging in a self-destructive behavior. During the first seven years of life we not only learn behaviors by watching other people, but we learn who we are as individuals. Children under seven years of age can't consciously conceive of who they are as a "self," as the EEG brain vibrations associated with consciousness isn't a predominate brain state. Instead, children of that age understand who they are by other people telling them "who they are." Imagine a parent telling their child, "You're the most wonderful, loving child. You can do anything you want..." Through hearing those words the child is downloading, "I'm loved. I'm a good person, I am capable." However, most parents are unaware that the words they say are directly recorded into the child's subconscious mind. Parents have a tendency to act as "coaches" in criticizing their children's negative behavior. They say things like, "You don't deserve this!" "Who do you think you are?" "You're not loveable!" However, children aged seven and under directly download the words with no consciousness as to what they mean. All they record is the message, "Not good enough." "You don't deserve that. You're not lovable." "Who do you think you are?" At least 80 percent of the people in our belief change workshops will not test positive to the belief statement, 'I love myself.' The problem is, if you can't love yourself, how can anybody else love you? This negative fate is largely because of all the critical assessment we receive as children.

Evolution

A consciousness evolution is occurring on the planet right now. Life on Earth has been wiped out five times via mass extinction. We're now in the sixth mass extinction phase on this planet, yet this one isn't due to asteroids hitting the Earth, but as a direct result of human behavior. The way we treat Mother Earth has been so destructive that we're undermining the web of life and we're essentially facing our own extinction. In the next few decades it has been predicted this world will go through some massive upheaval, the outcome of which hasn't yet been decided. For this reason, and to prevent our own destruction, it's essential that humanity adopts new sustainable behaviors.

The movie, The Matrix is not a science-fiction film, it's a documentary. We truly have been programmed. When we get out of the program and take the red pill, such as when we fall in love, there's literally another world out there.

We're not victims. We are creators of our life. However, we had no knowledge that we were programmed by other people. When we fall head over heels in love it's the same as taking the red pill as our creative conscious mind stays present and doesn't wander, resulting in a desired manifestation of Heaven on Earth.

Ways to reprogram the subconscious

Hypnosis

The conscious creative mind can learn in any number of ways, such as reading a book, but that information doesn't reach the subconscious mind because that mind isn't a creative mind. Hypnosis is one way that the subconscious mind learns, and one of the easiest ways of using hypnosis to change your life is to use subliminal tapes. Put earphones on at night when you go to bed and, as you drift off into sleep, you'll soon enter the theta vibration, which is the best brain state to reprogram your subconscious mind with new beliefs that serve you.

Repetition

After the age of seven, the subconscious mind learns through repetition. When you repeat something for long enough the mind will automatically create the accompanying program. When you first learn to drive you're overwhelmed with all the pedals and mirrors and gages and the people outside. But once you've learned to drive, you get in the car and you don't even think about any of that. You can even engage in conversations with your passengers as you drive along, without paying attention to the road. Your conscious mind focuses on the conversation, but it's the subconscious that's driving the car. Habituate new beliefs by repeating affirmations or new intentions frequently until they're downloaded into the mind.

Energy Psychology

There are fairly new processes called belief change modifications or energy psychology; these are essentially a form of super learning where you can rewrite a subconscious belief in five to ten minutes. Once you hit the record button you can download the data directly into the subconscious mind, just like you learned as an infant, without any effort at all.

There are a few steps to this process. Firstly, identify the belief you want to change. For example, if you're struggling with relationships, program the belief, "I love myself." If you don't love yourself no one else will be able to love you so you'll constantly sabotage relationships and then prove that you're not loveable. You could decide to program the statement, "I am loveable."

Do muscle testing to see if your mind supports that belief. The subconscious is the computer that controls muscle coordination and action. Make a statement with your conscious mind, such as "I love myself." Upon hearing that statement, the subconscious mind will probably communicate, based upon developmental programming, "No you don't!" This provokes a state of disharmony between the two minds. The weakening in the muscles of your arm tells you that the two minds aren't in agreement about the statement. This is an effective way of verifying what subconscious programs you have and checking whether your conscious and subconscious mind agree or don't agree before you begin working on a new belief or program. If your subconscious doesn't support the statement then you'll want to REprogram it. Prior to reprogramming the mind, it is first necessary to muscle test for "permission," asking your higher-self (spirit) if the intended change is in harmony with your life and asking the subconscious whether it is ready, willing and able to make the change. An inappropriate change in behavior could make your life worse!

Before the age of seven the brain's right and left hemispheres work in harmony with each other. They're synchronized. After the age of seven and throughout the rest of your life sometimes the right hemisphere is dominant and sometimes the left hemisphere is dominant. The right hemisphere is emotional and the left hemisphere is intellectual. Trying to introduce a new belief into a brain when the two hemispheres aren't in harmony is resisted by the brain. There are exercises that fire both hemispheres of the brain at the same time, causing them to run in synchrony. If you do these exercises, which involve crossing your legs and crossing your arms so that your right hand is on the left side of your body and your left hand is on the right, both hemispheres of the brain will be engaged, which is known as hemi-sync. If your disharmonious brain is in hemi-sync and you say, 'I love myself' you'll feel the disharmony right away. Then relax and say it again, and it will feel like less "static." The third time it will be even less static, and so on, until at some point you'll realize there's no resistance. To find out if the belief changed, muscle test again. If the belief changed, your arm will be strong. Once you've written a program or belief, it will stay put. The hardest part is deciding what statement to say that will bring you the results you're looking for. It's important to make a statement that even a five year old can understand. If you're not making enough money, rather than say "I want more money," which to a five year old may mean a few extra pennies, be specific and say, "I have an extra $100,000." Do not include the words intending the future, such as will, want, shall or desire into your statement, and make the statement in the present tense as if you have whatever you desire right now. Once a program is installed into the mind, such as, "I am healthy," the body may not be healthy at that point, but the function of the mind is to make the program real, so it will bring better health your way. The subconscious mind sees everything instantaneously—a bit like a chess player who sees ten moves ahead. If you program the subconscious mind appropriately it will lead you effectively and efficiently to your destination far faster and easier than your conscious mind ever could.

This process works so amazingly that I went from living in a strange, chaotic world to manifesting Heaven on Earth. I wasn't spiritual when I began my quest to understand cell biology. When I discovered that the cell's brain wasn't the nucleus but the membrane, I recognized that the function of the cell is controlled from the outside environment and each of us has a unique identifying set of receptors on our cells that distinguish our self from other selves. This made me realize that I, as an identity, was derived from an environmental signal. The "I" is not inside. When I realized my identity is derived from an external signal I realized my spiritual essence. I then asked myself a simple question, "Why have a spirit AND a body—why not just be a spirit?" I received the answer from my cells in the form of a question. "Bruce, if you're just a spirit, what does chocolate taste like?" And then it hit me…the body is a virtual-reality suit. We step into the body, and the body's cells, through biology and physical mechanisms, convert life experienced via the nervous system into vibrational signals. For example, light comes into our eye but the brain turns it into a vibrational broadcast. The same thing happens with taste, and all the other senses, as well as our emotions. Basically, our identity is picked up as a broadcast through a specific set of membrane self-receptors, and our life experiences are sent back to our source.

Most people think we die and our Soul goes to some special place called Heaven. I'd like to suggest a completely different consideration. We were born into Heaven to step into this virtual reality suit to create and experience life. When we're in the body we're enhancing the experience of spirit. Spirit can't taste chocolate, but the body can. We're here to create and enjoy life, and when we're not operating from the developmental programs, we create Heaven. We're wasting our "creative" lifetime thinking that if we follow all the religious principles then we'll get to Heaven when we die. To me, that's just a control mechanism. We came here to be creative and to sail the south sea and know what that's like. We've wasted a lot of our life unconsciously living other people's programming, destroying the environment in the process, and destroying ourselves. The current civilization can only maintain itself for as long as a large percentage of the population hold on to the existing system. The millennials (people under 40 years of age) now make up more than 50 percent of the population. They have a vision of a global world, and they're working to create new industries to turn the Earth back into a garden. It's predominantly the older generations who are holding on to old destructive beliefs, such as "survival of the fittest," and other limiting behaviors. Therefore, individually we must begin to understand how our lives can create harmony, and when seven billion people come together to create harmony, this planet will inevitably transform into Heaven on Earth. My wish for humanity and planet Earth is that we all change the belief of, "I am a victim" to, "I am a master who creates my life."

Light Practice

Here are some ways to change your subconscious beliefs (a more complete list is available under Resources at *www. brucelipton.com*). Research the available techniques and then take a step towards learning and implementing the one that resonates with you:

Psych-K

PSYCH-K is a set of principles and processes designed to change subconscious beliefs that limit the expression of your full potential as a Divine being having a human experience.

Emotional Freedom Technique

Based on impressive new discoveries regarding the body's subtle energies, Emotional Freedom Techniques (EFT) has been proven successful in thousands of clinical cases.

The Sedona Method

The Sedona Method is a unique, simple, powerful, easy-to-learn technique that shows you how to uncover your natural ability to let go of any painful or unwanted feeling, belief or thought.

Body Talk Systems

BodyTalk is a simple and effective form of therapy that allows the body's energy systems to be re-synchronized so they can operate as nature intended. BodyTalk can be used as a stand-alone system to treat many health problems, or seamlessly integrated into any health care system to increase its effectiveness and promote faster healing.

Heaven on Earth is a state of bliss, passion, energy, and health resulting from a huge love. Your life is so beautiful that you can't wait to get up to start a new day and thank the Universe that you are alive.

~Bruce Lipton

About Bruce Lipton

Bruce H. Lipton, scientist and lecturer, received his PhD at the University of Virginia in Charlottesville. He served as an associate professor of anatomy at the University of Wisconsin's School of Medicine. Lipton's research on mechanisms controlling cell behavior employed cloned human stem cells. In addition, he lectured in Cell Biology, Histology, and Embryology.

Bruce resigned his tenured position to pursue independent research integrating quantum physics with cell biology. His breakthrough studies on the cell membrane, the "skin" of the cell, revealed that the behavior and health of the cell was controlled by the environment, findings that were in direct contrast with prevailing dogma that life is controlled by genes.

Lipton returned to academia as a research fellow at Stanford University's School of Medicine to test his hypotheses (1987-1992). His ideas concerning environmental control were substantiated in two major scientific publications. The new research revealed the biochemical pathways connecting the mind and body and provided insight into the molecular basis of consciousness and the future of human evolution.

Bruce has taken his award-winning medical school lectures to the public and is currently a popular keynote speaker and workshop presenter on topics of conscious parenting and the science of complementary medicine.

For more information, *www.brucelipton.com*

Love and Be Loved

☼

By Dada J.P. Vaswani

*Love, love, love even thine enemy. And though he hate
thee as a thorn, thou wilt blossom, as a rose!*
~**Sadhu Vaswani**

Someone asked me once, "What is love?"
My reply was, "You will know when you become love!"
I believe in the strength and sustaining power of love:
not love that demands, expects, negotiates for something
in exchange—but unconditional love that offers itself in
understanding, sympathy, and compassion. Any other kind of
love can only be what the English call 'cupboard love;' which
may be a transaction, a bargain, but not the real thing. Love is
the most powerful healing force we have. My regret is that we
do not use it enough.

Many of us have a shallow and superficial conception of
love. We look upon love as something romantic. We regard it
as something intangible, ephemeral. Native American Indians
look upon love as a kind of wisdom. The famous writer Carlyle
echoed the same idea when he wrote, "A loving heart is the
beginning of all knowledge."

Today, people talk of hard skills, soft skills, communication
skills, and technical skills. May I tell you, life skills are more
important than professional skills! Love is far more essential to
a successful life than vocational degrees. For love purifies your
life and makes it sweet and meaningful.

It is difficult to define love or to describe it in words. And
yet you can know it when you feel it. The first love we feel is
the love of the mother. What is it that a mother will not do
for her children?

What is love?

What is love? This was the question put to Mansur when he was about to mount the scaffold. And he answered, "Love is not love until it renounces the I, the ego."

Renouncing the ego, you must move on and on until you have found what you seek—the Beloved within the heart. "For thy sake," sang Mansur. "I haste over land and water. Over the plain I pass, and the mountain I leave, and from everything I meet I turn my face, until the time when I reach that place where I am alone with Thee."

And then? What then? Listen to the words of Mansur:

> *I am He whom I love!*
> *And whom I love is I!*
> *We are two spirits in one body!*
> *When thou seest me, thou seest Him!*
> *And when Thou seest Him,*
> *Then thou seest us both!*

The way of love is selflessness. It is the way of sacrifice. Love has no place for ego or selfishness. Love is an ever-expanding positive energy. It was Rabindranath Tagore who said, "Love is an endless mystery, for it has nothing else to explain it." The greatest happiness in life is to love and be loved as we are.

Love is not possession. Love is not attachment. Love is above hate, envy, and jealousy. Love comes without any strings attached to it. Love is unconditional. Love is Divine. Love is pure energy. It is a flood of sublime thoughts.

Let me make it clear: when I talk about love, I do not refer to physical sensation or sexual attraction. One of the most admired women of the modern age, Helen Keller, said, "The best and most beautiful things in the world cannot be seen or even touched—they must be felt with the heart." True love is a feeling that touches mind, heart, and Soul. It is perhaps the feeling which is the highest that any human being is capable of. For I believe that love is of God. Love is not just an attribute of God—Love is God and God is Love! That is why I urge my young friends not to fall in love, but rise in true love—the love that helps and heals.

Love is not out there somewhere. It is with you, within you. The more you offer love to the world and the people in it, the more it will come back to you! Indeed, it was a wise man who asserted, "Love grows by giving. The love we give away is the only love we keep. The only way to retain love is to give it away."

The different forms of love

Love, they say, is a many splendored thing; love cannot be confined to 'romantic' love, erotic love, or indeed passionate love. What would life be like without parental love, family love, love for your siblings and children, love for nature and above all, love for God?

I do not wish to disparage romantic love or marital love: it is undoubtedly one of the finest aspects of love. When I hear people talk of 'love-at-first-sight,' I express the silent wish that this may include insight and foresight as well as hindsight. "Love happened in a flash!" young lovers often claim. If you don't want it to be just a flash-in-a-pan, you must grow in understanding and knowledge of each other.

Love is never blind, for love sees not only with the eyes, but the mind, the heart, and the spirit. Love goes about with wide open eyes, looking for opportunities to be of service to those in need.

God and love

Of a holy man, it is said that he was pained to see suffering and misery wherever he turned. In deep despair, he cried out to God, "O Lord! They call you the God of Love and Mercy. How can you bear to see so much suffering and yet do nothing about it?"

From the depth of his consciousness, he heard God's voice

tell him, "I did do something. I created you!" God has created us and poured love into our hearts so that we may alleviate the pain and suffering we see around us. Let us not curse the darkness. Let us kindle the Light of love in our hearts!

God loves you; He wants nothing but the best for you. If you ever doubt it, you have not yet realized the meaning of true love.

People who are overwhelmed by their problems often say to me, "If this is God's way of showing His love for me, well, thanks, but no thanks! He can keep it!"

Let me share with you this parable that tells us another way to look at problems. When God decided to send human beings as His children, down to this Earth, He gave each of them a carefully selected package of problems. He said to each child, with a smile, "These are yours, and yours alone. These problems bring with them very special blessings—and only you have the special talents and abilities to make these problems your servants."

God added softly, "Now go down to Earth. Know that I love you beyond measure. The problems I give you are a symbol of that love. The monument you make of your life with the help of your problems will be a symbol of your love for Me, your Heavenly Father. Go in peace—and be blessed!"

Seek God—not for material profit, but solely for His love!

Love and peace

Our hearts need to be saturated with love, for love is the Light which will illumine the world. For this, developed brains are not needed; we need enlightened hearts that can behold the vision of fellowship, unity, and brotherhood. Love is what we need to build a new humanity, a new world of brotherhood and peace. We must eliminate the dark forces of greed, selfishness, prejudice, and mistrust—and cultivate the power of Love, which is the secret power of a peaceful life and a peace-filled world!

The shortcut to world peace is through love, compassion, the spirit of caring and sharing, and service. It is also the shortest and quickest route to God. The way of service is closely allied to the way of brotherhood—for we need to assert, again and again, "I am my brother's keeper!"

There is a simple question that all saints ask of us: How can we claim our love to God if we do not love our fellow human beings? How can we call ourselves human beings if we watch our brothers and sisters suffering and struggling? Jesus said, "If a man says, I love God and hateth his brother, he is a liar, for if he loveth not his brother whom he hath seen, how can he love God whom he hath not seen?"

Love and humility go together. Wherever there is love, there is humility. They are but two sides of the same coin. Today science is marching on. Phenomenal advances have been made in medicine and electronic media. Spectacular strides have been made in exploring the moon and outer space. But we have not learned how to live together in amity and peace. There is an amusing incident in the life of the great Russian Leader, Maxim Gorkey. One day, he addressed a huge rally of peasants. He said to them, "Think of what science has done for you. Science has taught man how to fly in the air like a bird, and science has taught man how to swim in the ocean like a fish." Then a simple peasant said to the great leader, "Sir, what you say is too true. Science has taught man how to fly in the air like a bird and how to swim in the ocean like a fish, but science has not taught man how to live on the Earth in peace and amity with his fellow-men."

The opposite of love is not hate but indifference, or apathy—to the needs of those around you. We need to contribute our share—our mite—to the welfare of the world; to what Sri Krishna called lokasangraha.

I will tell you what I think is the price we must pay: We must love one another. I will go one step further: We must love each other or perish!

The first note on the musical scale of peace is LOVE—love as in the Commandment: Thou shalt love thy neighbor as thyself. It is this spirit of love that is expressed in the Universal bond of friendship. If we pick and choose and reject, Universal friendship does not have a chance! As Mother Teresa put it, "If you judge people, you have no time to love them."

Make no mistake about this, to an Indian, "Love thy neighbor" means loving the people of Pakistan; to an Israeli, "Love thy neighbor" means loving the Palestinians; to Christians, it means loving the Muslims and Hindus and Sikhs!

Let me remind you, therefore, of the words of the apostles:

"Bless them that curse you, and pray for your enemies. Fast on behalf of those that persecute you; for what thanks is there if you love them that love you? ...Do ye love them that hate you, and ye will not have an enemy!"

Can we, as human beings do this? If we could, we are asserting the Divinity in us—and we are helping to spread God's peace in the world!

Growing in love

How can we grow in the spirit of such true love? Let me offer you a few suggestions:

1. People often talk of 'falling' in love; you must rise in love—in love with God, and in love with your fellow human beings, as also with birds and animals. Therefore, establish a firm and loving relationship with God, first and foremost. Make God your father or mother, your friend or brother, or the Beloved of your heart. Let everything you do strengthen this relationship with God. When you have established such a relationship, you will find it natural to offer the love of your heart to everything and everyone around you.

I think the greatest affliction of modern civilization is that we are moving away from God, and the awareness that we are all His children. Some young atheists even say, "We have no need for God. There is nothing man cannot do on his own. Man has been able to set his foot on the moon. Man's rockets go flying past the distant planets. Man has been able to station satellites in space. Who needs God today?"

God is the source and sustainer of life. And man cannot live a healthy life physically, mentally, morally, spiritually, so long as he cuts himself off from God. It is very easy to drive the spirit out of the door—but once you have done that, life loses its flavour; the 'salt of life' grows flat.

May I share with you the prayer that I offer every day at the Lotus Feet of the Beloved? I urge you too, to turn to God as often as you can. Think of Him during your daily routine. Pray to Him every so often: *I love You God! I want to love You more and more! I want to love You more than anything else in the world. I want to love You to distraction, to intoxication. Grant me pure love and devotion for Thy Lotus Feet, and so bless me that this world-bewitching maya may not lead me astray. And make me, Blessed Master, an instrument of Thy help and healing in this world of suffering and pain.*

2. Speak softly; speak gently; speak with loving kindness. Treat everyone with love and respect. Greet God in everyone you meet.

3. Stop judging others, for true love is non-judgmental. Do not see the faults of others. When you find fault with others and criticize them harshly, you are drawing negative forces to yourself!

4. Love your family, love your friends and neighbours; but love those who hate you and criticize you as well! Breathe out love to those who ill-treat you and speak harshly to you! For every blow you receive, give back a blessing. This is not an impossible, impractical precept I'm preaching to you—it is a sound, wholesome approach to life that will bring lasting peace and happiness to you! "Love thine enemy," said Sadhu Vaswani, "and even though he hate thee as a thorn, thou shalt blossom as a rose."

5. Whatever you do, whatever you say, whatever you think, whatever you give, do it for the pure love of God! When you live life as an act of love and devotion to God, you will find that you can never do anything which will displease God! Your life will become the life beautiful; the life of love and purity.

There are a hundred and one ways of doing the same thing. Are you a professor teaching in a classroom? Are you a lawyer arguing a case in a court of law? Are you a doctor attending to patients? There are many ways of doing the same thing. Some are right, some are wrong. But only one is the best! And because you are doing everything for the love of God, because you are doing everything as an offering unto the Lord, you must do your work in the best way possible.

6. Learn to forgive others who have harmed you or hurt you in any way. Forgive before they even ask for your forgiveness. The 'F' of forgiveness is Freedom—freedom from negative emotions, grudges, resentments, and bitterness. When these 'blockages' are cleared from your emotional arteries, love flows through your life effortlessly and freely.

7. True love is not attachment or possessiveness. Attachment of any kind, as the Gita tells us, leads to suffering. Raga, or abhinivesha (clinging and attachment) as it is called, is an impediment—not only on the path of liberation, but also in the attainment of personal happiness. On the other hand, detachment is one of life's greatest lessons for those who seek the true joy of life. In the words of the inspired poet, "If you love someone very dearly, give him wings: let him fly!"

8. The law of love is the law of service and sacrifice. Therefore, go out of your way to help others. And rejoice in everything that the Will of God brings to you.

Love blesses the one who offers it and the one who receives it. Love can keep you healthy and happy, and help you face the problems of daily life in the right spirit! Learn to love the good qualities that you are capable of manifesting. Learn to love Truth, purity, humility, sacrifice, service, honesty, and gratitude. Choose one quality each day and focus your loving attention on it. Love other people who express that quality and learn from them.

Above all, keep on smiling. Smile all the while. Smile at each other, smile at your spouse, smile at your siblings, smile at your children, smile at your friends and friends-to-be—there are no strangers, there are only friends-to-be—and that will help you to grow in love for each other. And never forget that paradise is where love dwells and where people keep on smiling at each other.

Light Practice: Meditation on Universal Love and peace

Step 1: Sit in a relaxed posture. As far as possible, the back, the neck, and the head should be in a straight line. In the beginning you may find it difficult to bring them all in a straight line, but do it as far as possible. Above all, be relaxed. Relax your body, relax your muscles, relax your limbs. Make sure you are seated comfortably and focused inward.

Step 2: Now visualize a beautiful landscape; a tranquil scene before your mind's eye. It may be the silver waters of the sea on a calm, moonlit night; it may be a majestic mountain peak capped with virgin snow; it may be the dark green, cool and shady interiors of the woods in the springtime; it may be the misty, verdant slopes of a hillside—imagine any scene that has been long held in your mind as a precious memory, or recalled from a picture you may have seen, which fills you with a sense of peace and joy. Close your eyes and picture yourself there, in your favorite location. Feel the peace and tranquillity all around you. Let it enter your heart and Soul and permeate every pore of your being.

Step 3: Now take deep rhythmic breaths. Be conscious of every breath you take. As you breathe in, tell yourself that you are inhaling the peace of God, the peace that passeth, surpasseth understanding. As you breathe out, you are exhaling calmness all around. There is peace within you, and calm all around you. Reflect on this beautiful passage from the Vedas:

May there be peace in the higher regions; may there be peace in the firmament; may the waters flow peacefully; may all the Divine powers bring unto us peace. The Supreme Lord is Peace. May we all dwell in peace, peace, peace, and may that peace come into each of us.

You are now in an environment of serenity and peace. You may, if you like, imagine yourself seated on a rock in the midst of an ocean. Waves arise. They dash against the rock. The rock stands still and sturdy, unaffected, calm, tranquil, peaceful, and serene. Waves arise. Waves are the distracting thoughts. They dash against the rock. The rock of your mind is unaffected, calm, tranquil, peaceful, and serene.

You now begin to realize your oneness with All That Is, all men, all creatures, all things, all conditions. You are not apart from others. The others and you are parts of the one great whole. You are in every man, in every woman, in every child. You are in every unit of life, in every bird and animal, in every fowl and fish, in every insect, in every shrub, in every plant. You belong to all countries and communities, all races and religions. You are at one with the Universe. As you become aware of this oneness of all creation, you find your heart filled with loving kindness and a spirit of kinship and compassion with all things and all beings in this vast and wonderful world.

Step 4: And now we come to the crucial, final stage of this meditation. In this stage, you breathe out love, peace and happiness, goodwill and bliss to all. May all be happy and full of peace and bliss. Think of all who dwell in the Northern lands and pray in the heart within: "May all who dwell in the Northern lands be happy and full of peace and bliss." Then think of all who dwell in the Southern lands and offer the prayer, "May all who dwell in the Southern lands be happy and full of peace and bliss." Likewise, "May all who dwell in Eastern lands and all who dwell in Western lands, be happy and full of peace and bliss."

Breathe out love, peace, and goodwill to all. May all be happy and full of peace and bliss. All living things whether they be near or far, big or tiny, rich or poor, educated or illiterate, whether they be born or are still in the womb unborn, may all, all, all be happy and full of peace and bliss. May those that love you and those that for some reason or the other are unable to love you, may those that speak well of you, and those that for some reason or the other are unable to speak well of you, may all, all, all, without exception, be happy and full of peace and bliss. You are in them all. It is only when they become happy that you are happy. May all be free from disease, ignorance, and sorrow.

Step 5: Open your eyes gently and feel love and peace infusing your body, mind, heart, and Soul.

As you get up from this meditation, you will find that you yourself are happy and full of peace and bliss!

Positive Affirmations of Love

Recite these affirmations at times throughout the day when you feel to:

Love is never blind. Love sees with the eyes of the heart.

Love is unconditional. It does not come with strings attached.

Love is not a bargaining tool or a blackmail weapon. It cannot be subject to conditions or stipulations.

A loving relationship is the greatest gift a human being can be blessed with.

God's love for us manifests itself in a thousand ways, every minute, every hour, every day!

Exercises in Love

Just for today, don't try to 'influence' or 'persuade' or 'reason with' people you meet; instead, offer your loving support and understanding to them. You will find that this brings out the best in them.

Today, choose one person who means the most to you. And just for today, look at everything you do from that person's perspective. Just for today put that person's interest above your own.

Make a list of all the things, the people, and the qualities that you love the most. Now, set your priorities. What or whom do you wish to love more than all else? Make a resolution to devote more energy and effort to fostering those relationships that mean the most to you

True love is sacrificial. It is in giving, not in getting; in losing, not in gaining; in releasing not in possessing that we love!

~**Dada Vaswani**

About Rev. Dada J.P. Vaswani

Dada J. P. Vaswani is one of India's greatly beloved and revered spiritual leaders. He is the life-force at the helm of the renowned Sadhu Vaswani Mission, an international, non-profit, social welfare and service organization with its headquarters in Pune, and active centers all over the world.

Born in 1918, at Hyderabad-Sind, Dada was a brilliant scholar, who turned his back on a promising academic career to devote himself to his uncle and Guru, Sadhu Vaswani, a highly revered modern day saint. Today, the Master's mantle has fallen on Dada, whom devotees and admirers look upon as the representative of God on Earth, a mentor and guardian of their deepest values and spiritual aspirations.

Not only does Dada express the most profound Truths in the simplest terms, but he lives and acts these Truths in deeds of everyday life. He lives his religion and spirituality bearing witness to his ideals in thought, word, and deed, thus offering a tremendous source of inspiration to everyone who meets him, even once in a lifetime.

A fluent, powerful, and witty speaker, and an inspired writer who has authored over 150 books and booklets, Dada is the youngest 97-year-old that you can ever meet.

For more information, *www.sadhuvaswani.org*

Compassion

Teachings of His Holiness the Dalai Lama
Written by Keidi Keating

Our human compassion binds us the one to the other—
not in pity or patronizingly, but as human beings who
have learnt how to turn our common suffering into hope
for the future.

~Nelson Mandela

All humans want a happy life, and none of us want to experience suffering. It is our basic right to feel joy. In fact, any form of life, including plants and animals, has the right to not only exist, but exist with happiness.

Happiness and joyfulness are felt mainly on the sensory level. On the mental level, we humans are far more complex because of our intelligence, which creates the capacity to remember events that happened in the past. We also have the capacity to visualize and imagine the future. However, that causes a greater disturbance and distance in our mind.

Once I attended a meeting in Frankfurt, Germany. There were people present from many different cultures. A representative from Native America delivered a long speech, and his message was that as white people killed Native Americans in the past, now all white people should move out of America. He had developed that point of view due to something which happened centuries ago. As a result he was a very unhappy man, and because of the past memory, plus the ability of his imagination, he had created a great disturbance and distance in his mind.

As humans, even if everything is okay in the here and now, we still tend to worry about tomorrow, about next week, about next year, about next decade. Or we think too much about past events, and through that imagination our present sense of calmness is completely destroyed.

Usually, when we face problems we look at them only from our own point of view, which often leads to negative consequences. It is important for us to have a broader perspective, and look at situations from all angles. Every event has different aspects. When we look at the same event from a certain viewpoint we are able to see something different.

Lust, hatred, and anger narrow our outlook, which makes true compassion impossible. An experienced psychotherapist once told me that when we generate anger 90 percent of the ugliness of the object of our anger is due to our own exaggeration. This can be avoided by seeing the fuller picture.

Religion

For the last three-thousand years human society has worshipped various religious faiths. Interestingly, all religions carry the same message of love, forgiveness, compassion, tolerance, contentment, self-discipline, and so on. Today, there are some people who still feel the value of religious faith, and there is an equal portion of society that has no interest in religion. Sometimes there is a tendency to look at the role of religion in extreme terms. For example, people recognize the value of compassion and other morals, and feel that they therefore must embrace religion as the foundation of that. That is one extreme. The other stand is, 'Because I have no interest in religion myself I should not pay serious attention to values such as love, compassion, and forgiveness.' Religious advocates often believe that moral ethics must be based on some form of religious faith. I think that point of view is too narrow. And then there are another group of people who believe that there must be a third way, having no religious belief but promoting human values, such as compassion, loving, and forgiveness. Some of my Muslim friends interpret this as a rejection of religion, but according to the Indian way, it does not mean rejecting religion but respecting all religions, and also respecting non-believers. My earnest request is that you practice compassion whether you believe in religion or not.

Biased

When our minds are clouded by hatred, selfishness, jealousy, and anger, we not only lose control, we lose our sense of judgment. Our own destructive emotions pollute our outlook. We must cleanse our internal perspective through the practice of compassion. When unfavorable conditions are removed with hatred, that creates its own problems because hatred, distorted by its bias, does not see the true situation.

Real compassion extends to each and every sentient being, not just to friends and family, or those who face terrible situations. True compassion is offered to even those who wish to harm us. We must learn to be grateful to our enemies for they are our gurus and teachers.

When you develop an affinity for all sentient beings and the desire that they should all have happiness, such a desire is valid because it is unbiased. However, our present compassion being limited to friends and family is heavily influenced by ignorant attachment, and as such it is biased.

The narrow minded worldly life is characterized by 'the eight worldly concerns:'
Like / Dislike
Gain / Loss
Praise / Blame
Fame / Disgrace

The worldly way of life is to be unhappy when the four unfavorable concerns happen to our self or our friends, but to be pleased when they happen to our enemies. Whereas true love and compassion are based not on actions but on the crucial fact that all other sentient beings want happiness and do not want suffering, just as you do, which makes everyone equal.

Once you put the emphasis on their similarity with yourself, compassion has a solid foundation that does not vacillate depending on temporary circumstances.

In my own practice, when I consider, for instance, a particular person who is currently torturing Tibetans in my homeland, I do not concentrate on that person's bad attitude and bad behavior. Instead I reflect on the fact that this is a human being who, like me, wants happiness and does not want suffering; through ignorance this person is bringing pain to himself or herself and destroying their own happiness as well as that of others. Looking at things from this perspective, my response is love and compassion. If I considered the person harming Tibetans as my enemy, I could not have compassion as my response.

Truly altruistic people have concern for limitless number of sentient beings without any consideration of friend or foe, nationality or ethic group, and this compassion extends to each and every type of suffering.

In a sense all human beings belong to a single family. We need to embrace the oneness of humanity and show concern for everyone—not just *my* family, or *my* continent. Differences of religion, race, economic system, and government are all secondary.

No matter how important you may be, you are only a single person. To lose the happiness of a single person is important, but not as important as losing the happiness of many other beings. The aim of human society must be the compassionate betterment of all from one moment to the next.

I believe there are many levels of compassion of varying degrees of intensity and strength. Like any emotion, it is not independent or absolute. Some emotions interlink due to different factors. Sometimes you may have a sense of concern, but you also feel more superior than the other person. That is not genuine compassion. Compassion means respecting another person's right to be happy, and recognizing that the other person is just like you. Another kind of compassion you feel may be entirely dependent on the other's attitude. That kind of compassion is mixed with attachment, and based on another's action. As soon as their attitude changes even slightly, you also change your attitude immediately. These feelings of compassion are also limited and biased. Genuine compassion is not based on the person's attitude, but recognizing that they, like me, also want happiness and not suffering. When we reach that place inside, we have the capacity to touch even our enemies with genuine compassion.

Materialism and attachment

We are overly attached to superficialities and material possessions, yet the day will come when we will no longer be here on Earth and we will leave all our physical things behind. It's important to remember that this could happen at any time so be mindful that what we gather will eventually disperse. By cultivating an awareness of death we are more likely to refrain from actions that will harm both our present and our future.

Generally we are content with slight amounts of spiritual practice and progress, but materially we always want more and more. Ideally, it should be the other way around. If we seek contentment externally it will never come. Therefore, try to be satisfied with adequate food, clothing, and shelter.

When finery and money become more important than spiritual development, distressing emotions increase. When you notice an attachment starts to develop, try to find negative qualities in the object of your desire.

Ordinary love and compassion are intertwined with attachment because their motivations are selfish. However, if love and compassion thrive alongside the clear recognition of the importance of the rights of others, they will reach even those who may do you harm. In order to be more open minded and holistic, we need to practice detachment.

Wherever I go I share with people that we are all human beings, and we all want a happy and successful life. However, success and happiness largely depend on our mental attitude. Materially perhaps we are successful and we have a lot of money and fame, and maybe we also have an abundance of friends, but the question is are they genuine friends or are they friends of money and power? Often those who have more money and power have more friends. And similarly, those with less money and power have less friends. When someone's fortune increases they tend to be very happy for a while. And then their fortunes decreases and when they phone their friends, suddenly there is no answer! These are not genuine friends, but artificial friends; they are friends of power.

It's crucial to use our awareness to analyze what emotions bring us a greater sense of inner peace, and, at the same time, to know what emotions disturb our peace of mind. We need food, clothes, shelter, and external things in order to survive. We choose what clothing to wear and what food to eat. Since our inner state of being is also dependent on measuring our happiness, it is equally important to analyze the nature of different emotions, such as anger, hatred, and jealousy, and choose wisely what virtues we allow into our reality.

Self-discipline

Self-confidence is the opposition force of fear. In order to reduce fear, we must be more confident, which brings us more positive will. Therefore, compassion brings us inner strength, and reduces fear and insecurity. On the physical level anxiety and frustrations are very bad for the basic elements of the body. When our mind is calm and at peace these bodily elements run smoothly, as they were designed. However, worry, fear, stress, and anxiety disturb our bodily elements. Some scientists say that anger actually eats away at our human system. On the other hand, emotions such as compassion, strengthen our immune system. Among the many different emotions some are destructive and negative, while some are constructive and positive. We would be wise to put some effort into increasing the positive emotions and reducing the negative emotions. There's no way to cure disturbances on the mental level by relying purely on external means, such as taking drugs, drinking alcohol, and so on. Temporary methods often create even more confusion in our mind. Nevertheless, through a certain way of thinking, and by training our mind, we can reduce disturbances in our mind and sustain a greater level of calmness and satisfaction, in spite of difficult events and situations.

Resolve to use this lifetime in this body effectively. Use your fleeting life for your benefit and that of others through self-discipline and taming the mind.

The great Indian scholar-yogi Dharmakirti said, "The nature of the mind is clear Light; defilements are superficial." We call this basic consciousness the fundamental inborn mind of clear Light. Because it makes transformation possible it's also called our inner nature of enlightenment. It exists at the root of all consciousness. This means that you are already equipped with the basic quality needed to attain complete enlightenment— the luminous and cognitive nature of your own mind. All of us already have some level of compassion, despite differences in its development.

Develop an ability to watch your thoughts. Be a mental observer. Then your mind will be able to step outside of anger and you will recognize what is called 'ordinary mind,' which is unaffected by the liking and not liking, wanting and not wanting.

Consciousness is luminous in the sense that its nature is clear and that it illuminates or reveals, like a lamp that dispels darkness so that objects may be seen. The luminous nature of the mind is not diminished even by afflictive emotions, such as hatred. When the mind is not fractured into many different functions, it's natural state of luminous knowing can be recognized, and if you stay with it, the experience of luminosity and knowing will increase. When this happens, hatred will gradually melt into the nature of consciousness.

When our self-defeating attitudes, emotions, and conceptions cease, so will the harmful actions arising from them. You do not have to stop the various thoughts and feelings that dawn to the mind; just do not get caught up in them. The mind will then take its own natural form and the basic purity of its clear Light can emerge and be known. Some ways you can help this process are to:

Stop remembering what happened in the past.

Stop thinking about what might happen in the future.

Let the mind flow of its own accord without the overlay of thought. Observe it for a while in its natural state.

Wonderful spiritual qualities, such as unconditional love and compassion are all present in basic form in our diamond mind: their manifestation is only prevented by certain temporary conditions.

When you have a strong sense of concern about others you may still get little disturbances in your life, but there is a big difference between one's own suffering and the disturbance of another's suffering.

Developing compassion is a process

Transformation of inner attitudes cannot be attained without working hard at it. A gradual approach is far better than trying to jump too high too soon. You will gradually notice changes in your reactions to individuals and the world. Under no circumstances should you lose hope. Do not give up. If you are pessimistic you cannot possibly succeed.

You may be rich, powerful, and well-educated but without healthy feelings of kindness and compassion there will be no peace within yourself, and no peace within your family. Cultivating an attitude of compassion is a slow process. As you gradually internalize it day by day, year by year, like a huge piece of ice in the water, the mass of your problems will gradually melt away.

Benefits of compassion

There are seven billion human brothers and sisters on this planet, so everywhere we go we meet new people, but there are no differences between us. If you are honest, open, and sincere people respond in kind. I've met people who initially were a little reserved or distant, yet within a few minutes their attitude changed and they became much happier. When someone takes this attitude of compassion seriously it automatically creates a friendly atmosphere wherever they go. A person who practices compassion and forgiveness has much more inner strength than those who choose not to.

When we are calmer and happier our daily mood has the potential to be more positive. And then, even when we receive bad news in our life, our basic mental attitude is good and we have a certain inner strength. Negative news or events still bring some unhappiness or shock, but deep down our mind remains calm with less disturbance. Like an ocean, the waves are sometimes strong, sometimes weak, but underneath the ocean it always remains calm.

Morality, compassion, decency, and wisdom are the building blocks of all civilizations. These virtues must be cultivated in childhood and sustained through systematic moral education in a supportive social environment, so a more humane world may emerge. Each of us has a responsibility out of love and compassion for humankind to seek harmony among nations, cultures, ethnic groups, and economic and political systems. As we truly come to recognize the oneness of all humankind our motivation to find peace will grow stronger.

Love, compassion, and the concern for others are the real sources of happiness. With these in abundance you will not be disturbed by even the most uncomfortable circumstances. If we really want happiness, we must widen the sphere of love.

World suffering

Conflicts such as bloodshed, problems arising out of nationalism and national boundaries are all manmade. If we looked down at the world from space, we would not see any demarcations of national boundaries. We would simply see one small planet. Once we draw a line in the sand we develop the feeling of 'us' and 'them.' Caring for our neighbor's interests is essentially caring for our own future. In harming our enemy we ourselves are harmed.

When we encounter human suffering we must respond with compassion rather than question the politics of those we help. Instead of asking whether their country is a friend or an enemy, we must think, these are human beings, they are suffering, and they have a right to happiness equal to our own.

After first understanding your own situation and then seeking to hold yourself back from suffering, extend your realization to other beings and develop compassion, dedicating yourself to holding others back from suffering.

Anger

Conflicts in the world arise from a failure to understand how much we have in common. Hatred and fighting cannot bring happiness to anyone, even those who win. Attempts by global powers to dominate one another through violence are clearly counterproductive. More dangerous than guns and bombs are hatred, lack of compassion, and lack of respect for the rights of others. External peace is impossible without internal peace. Anger and egoism are the most dangerous weapons for they lead to manipulating others. We must minimize anger and cultivate kindness and a warm heart through spiritual training.

Some human beings become slaves of anger, and as a result they don't only harm other people but they also lose their own peace of mind. Therefore, we have several reasons to feel concern about them. Acting aggressively, out of a place of anger, is a sign of weakness. Anger means people feel threatened or anxious, which is weakness, whereas compassion is a sign of strength.

Anger cannot be overcome by anger. If you control your anger and show its opposite—compassion, and love—you remain in peace and gradually the anger of the other will also diminish. When someone is trying to take advantage of you, remember this other person is a human being and has a right to be happy.

An insecure person does not fare well when faced with negative situations. For example, if someone has a fight with their partner and the next day their mood is still affected. For these people, even the slightest disturbance in their life causes them to immediately burst. Therefore, a calm mind is very important. One way to deal with this is that when a feeling of strong anger arrives, in that moment, oppose the force of anger and stimulate kindness and calmness instead. It's difficult, but it's the wise way.

Think of one another as true brothers and sisters, deeply concerned with another's welfare. Seek to lessen the suffering of others. Rather than working solely to acquire wealth we have to do something meaningful. The whole world is a part of you. Foolish people only think of themselves and the result is always negative. Wise people think of others, helping them as much as they can, and the result is happiness.

The three steps to compassion

First Step: In the first step toward compassion we must develop our empathy or closeness to others, and recognize the gravity of their misery. It is also important that we reflect upon the kindness of others, which is a fruit of cultivating empathy. We must recognize how our fortune is really dependent upon the cooperation and contributions of others. Every aspect of our present well-being is due to hard work on the part of others. As we look around at the buildings we live in and work in, the roads we travel, the clothes we wear, or the food we eat, we must acknowledge that all these are provided by others. None of this would exist for us to enjoy and make use of were it not for the kindness of so many people unknown to us. As we contemplate in this manner, our appreciation for others grows, as does our empathy and closeness to them.

Second Step: The next important practice is recognizing the suffering of others. It tends to be more powerful and effective if we focus on our own suffering and then extend that recognition to the suffering of others. Our compassion for others grows as our recognition of their suffering does. We all naturally sympathize with someone who is undergoing the manifest suffering of physical illness or the loss of a loved one. It is more difficult to feel compassion for someone experiencing what Buddhists refer to as 'the suffering of change,' which in conventional terms means pleasurable experiences, such as the enjoyment of fame or wealth. When we see people enjoy such worldly success, instead of feeling compassion because we know it will eventually end, leaving them to experience disappointment at their loss, often our reaction is to feel admiration and sometimes even envy. If we had a genuine understanding of suffering and its nature, we would recognize how the experience of fame and wealth are temporary and how the pleasure they bring will naturally end, causing one to suffer.

Third Step: There is also a third and more profound level of suffering, which is the most subtle. We experience this suffering constantly as it is a by-product of cyclical existence. We are continuously under the control of negative emotions and thoughts. And, as long as we are under their control, our very existence is a form of suffering. This level of suffering pervades our lives, sending us round and round in vicious circles of negative emotions and non-virtuous actions. However, this form of suffering is difficult to recognize. It is not the evident state of misery we find in the suffering of suffering. Nor is it the opposition of our fortune and well-being, as we see in the suffering of change. Nevertheless, this pervasive suffering is the most profound. It permeates all aspects of life.

Once we have cultivated a profound understanding of the three levels of suffering in our own experience it is easier to shift the focus onto others and reflect upon the three levels. From there we can develop the wish that other beings are freed of all suffering.

Compassion enables us to refrain from thinking in a self-centered way. We experience great joy and never fall to the extreme of simply seeking our own personal happiness and salvation. We continually strive to develop and perfect our virtue and wisdom. With such compassion, we shall eventually possess all the necessary conditions for attaining enlightenment. We must therefore cultivate compassion from the very start of our spiritual practice.

If, in the midst of the garbage of lust, hatred, and ignorance—emotions that afflict our minds and our world—we generate a compassionate attitude, we should cherish this. After all, compassion is a priceless jewel.

Light Practice

When you see people suffering make the following wish enthusiastically from the depths of your heart:

This person is suffering very badly, and despite wanting to gain happiness and alleviate suffering, does not know how to give up non-virtues and adopt virtues. May his or her suffering, as well as its causes, ripen within me.

This is called the practice of 'taking the suffering of others within yourself using the instrument of compassion.'

You can also imagine the following:

I will give to these sentient beings, without the slightest hesitation or regret, whatever virtues I have accumulated in the form of good karma, which will be auspicious for them.

This is called 'the practice of giving away your own happiness using the instrument of love.'

Perform these practices along with the inhalation and exhalation of breath—inhaling the others' pain and exhaling your own happiness into their lives.

If you want others to be happy, practice compassion. If you want to be happy, practice compassion.
~His Holiness, the Dalai Lama

*This chapter was written by Keidi Keating directly from the teachings and words of His Holiness the Dalai Lama, which were extracted from his books and speeches on the subject of Compassion.

About His Holiness the Dalai Lama

His Holiness the 14th Dalai Lama, Tenzin Gyatso, is the spiritual leader of Tibet yet he describes himself as a simple Buddhist monk. He was born on July 6, 1935, to a farming family, in a small hamlet located in north-eastern Tibet. At the age of two, the child who was named Lhamo Dhondup at that time, was recognized as the reincarnation of the previous 13th Dalai Lama, Thubten Gyatso.

The Dalai Lamas are believed to be manifestations of Avalokiteshvara or Chenrezig, the Bodhisattva of Compassion and the patron saint of Tibet. Bodhisattvas are believed to be enlightened beings who have postponed their own nirvana and chosen to take rebirth in order to serve humanity.

In 1950 His Holiness was called upon to assume full political power after China's invasion of Tibet in 1949/50. In 1954, he went to Beijing for peace talks with Chinese leaders. But finally, in 1959, with the brutal suppression of the Tibetan national uprising in Lhasa by Chinese troops, His Holiness was forced to escape into exile. Since then he has been living in Dharamsala, northern India.

In 1989 His Holiness was awarded the Nobel Peace Prize for his non-violent struggle for the liberation of Tibet. He has consistently advocated policies of non-violence, even in the face of extreme aggression.

His Holiness has received more than 150 awards and prizes in recognition of his message of peace, non-violence, inter-religious understanding, Universal responsibility, and compassion. He has authored or co-authored more than 110 books.

For more information, *www.dalailama.com*

Non-Duality: the Enlightened Darkness

By Jeff Foster

Wisdom says, 'I am nothing.'
Love says, 'I am everything.'
Between the two, my life flows.
~**Nisargadatta Maharaj**

In the famous Chinese Yin-Yang symbol, where Light and dark make up two halves of a greater whole, something amazing happens: a small dark circle appears in the light region, and a small light circle appears in the dark region. Light and dark, those seemingly 'ultimate' opposites, are therefore not really 'opposites' at all—in reality they do not oppose each other, but complement and sustain each other, support and penetrate each other. They give life to each other. That is the secret. Light sees itself in dark, and dark sees itself in Light—a beautiful relationship, a cosmic co-operation. At the heart of reality, there is no war. The war only exists in the human mind.

In the past, we were taught to think of spiritual enlightenment as purification: the removal of darkness and the victory of Light, the death of spiritual impurity. We saw enlightenment as some kind of goal or destination, a final resting place at the end of a long journey, somewhere to reach in the future. Some people saw enlightenment as a special spiritual state, or an experience that would happen one day, if they meditated deeply enough, or worshipped their guru hard enough, or gave away all their possessions and destroyed their ego. Some people imagined that enlightenment only happened to very lucky or special people, or that it had something to do with karma or grace. So many spiritual teachers spoke about enlightenment in so many different ways, that it all became confusing for a mind genuinely looking for answers.

I have come to see that the word 'enlightenment' is pointing to something very simple, obvious, and readily available to everyone. Enlightenment is not a superhuman achievement, but present in each and every moment, if you have eyes to see it. It's not something that happens to you one day, and it's not a goal or a final destination for a seeker. It's more like a subtle shift in perspective, a remembering of who you really are, a clear seeing of what's right in front of you.

My story

Years ago, I had become totally obsessed with spiritual enlightenment. I wanted it so badly. I wanted to be 'an enlightened person,' so my pain, my anxiety, my intense shyness, and my sickening depression would come to an end. I wanted freedom, release from the burden of being a 'self,' a separate 'me' in a big bad world, and I saw enlightenment as the ultimate solution.

I did everything I could in order to bring this transformation about. I meditated for many hours a day, read every book I could get my hands on, watched every YouTube video I could find from every enlightened master, and self-inquired until I was blue in the face. I contorted my body into strange positions, became a vegan, and stared at photos of enlightened people for hours. Ordinary life was just not interesting or relevant for me any longer—I wanted the Ultimate, the Absolute, the Pinnacle. I wanted to escape this ordinary life and reach the extraordinary. Then I would be able to rest, finally rest.

I shut myself off from the world—my friends, my family, worldly pleasures. I spent long summer days indoors, meditating, focusing, trying to understand the ultimate Truth of existence. I began to have all kinds of what we might call 'spiritual experiences'—experiences of total uninterrupted bliss, ecstatic visions, travels to other realms, incredible insights. Back then, that's what I thought spirituality was all about: seeking and maintaining amazing experiences. As the experiences became more and more intense, I thought I was getting closer and closer to the 'finish line.'

But I soon began to realize something amazing: even the most incredible, blissful, orgasmic spiritual experiences have a beginning and an ending. However wonderful an experience was, however intense or exciting, however powerful, it would soon pass. No experience seemed to be permanent. Every experience, every insight, every blissful feeling would come, last for a while, and then go. The greatest pleasure, the most dramatic insights, they would all eventually slip through my fingers like sand. I was always waiting, hoping, yearning for that final experience, that ultimate experience that would sustain itself, the one that would never pass, that would end all my suffering once and for all. But it never came, no matter how hard I tried. I couldn't seem to reach that ultimate 'state' that the gurus spoke about.

New questions started to become alive in me: How could a self actually let go of a self, awaken from itself, free itself from itself? How could an ego become ego-free? The paradoxes started to pile up, and drive me mad. Was there such a thing as enlightenment after all? Had the spiritual gurus been misleading me? And why was I always running away from the present moment, trying to reach a future goal that never seemed to arrive? Why was I always dissatisfied with life? Was there something fundamentally broken in my psyche? Was I doomed to spiritual failure? And who was the one asking all these difficult questions? Who was the one who longed for freedom? Who was I, before I thought about myself?

Discovering the answer

One day, I was lying in bed, on the verge of giving up on life completely. I had become totally exhausted, frazzled, and disillusioned with all this spiritual seeking, with all the questions, with all the paradoxes, the complicated spiritual philosophies, with all the beautiful words of all the gurus and teachers. I was tired of the whole damn thing. "I'm never going to get there," I said to myself. In fact, I didn't even know where "there" was anymore. What was I actually looking for? I didn't know. And yet, I couldn't give up, either. A fire had started within me that I couldn't extinguish. A fire for Truth, for reality, for freedom. Yet everything I was doing to become awakened seemed to make me feel less awakened than ever. A double bind. When would peace come? When would I be able to rest? The questions were so close, yet the answers seemed so far away. Then, for some reason, I glanced over at a chair. It was not a remarkable chair—it was a chair that I'd seen thousands of times before; a chair that had been there since I was a child. A tatty brown chair; an old friend. And suddenly, I remembered something, something familiar, something that had always been on the tip of my tongue: *everything I have ever been looking for is right here.*

Don't get me wrong. I hadn't 'attained' anything with this insight. This was more like a falling away of the whole need to 'attain' anything in the first place, a falling in love with the present moment. There was no big drama, no fireworks, no dramatic experience, no spiritual 'high,' there was just a simple and quiet knowing: the extraordinary lies in the ordinary. No experience was ever needed other than the present experience. Every breath was a miracle! The carpet was a miracle. My body was a miracle. The chair was a miracle. In fact, it wasn't really a 'chair' at all—'chair' was just a word I'd learned and repeated throughout my life. It was life itself, appearing temporarily as a chair. It was oneness, the One Life behind all there is and is not, disguised as an ordinary chair. It was that which I'd always been seeking, disguised as something so very ordinary. No wonder I'd missed the miracle my whole life. I had been looking for it.

Knowing

This recognition didn't come in words, of course; it wasn't the dualistic mind, the mind of opposites, that was understanding all this. This was a knowing that came before language, before concepts. It was like seeing the world with fresh eyes, with the innocence of a child. All my spiritual seeking had been in vain, in a sense. I'd been like a wave in the ocean desperately seeking the ocean. I'd been looking for something I would never find, because it was already here, and I was already it. I had been so innocent though, in my misunderstanding of the Universe. I began weeping, grieving over all my old ideas about life and myself. I couldn't believe I'd never seen this before: the miracle of the ordinary, the simple gift of being alive. With all my cleverness, with all my intellectual prowess, I'd missed what had been right under my nose. So obvious that a child could see it. There was a sense of humility though, deep gratitude, and a willingness to never forget this ancient Truth.

I realized that I'd always been looking outside of myself for happiness and contentment. I'd been looking outwards: to other people, demanding that they make me happy. I'd been looking to objects, possessions, substances, things that are ever-changing. I'd been looking to worldly success, popularity, fame, and in the end, even spiritual enlightenment. I'd been projecting my happiness 'out there,' in the future. And all the while, I'd never really been present. I'd never shown up for my life, savored the preciousness of every living moment. Spirituality had become another escape for me; always seeking, always chasing after the next 'high,' rather than falling in love with what was present and alive. I had been addicted to the future, addicted to spiritual attainments.

I started wandering around the house, still weeping like a baby, looking at everything afresh, seeing the ordinary things of life with eyes wide open. A carpet. A refrigerator. A carrot. A fly buzzing around. A flower in a vase. Everything was so fresh, so alive, so 'here,' a miracle beyond words. It was like seeing the world without the heavy story of 'Jeff,' without his history and his future projections, seeing life without the seeker, without the questioner, seeing the incredible fullness of the world. The chair, the carpet, my clothes, even a bit of mould growing in the corner of the bathroom, everything was so alive and fresh. Everything was a glorious expression of the One Life, and always had been. And I had no way of separating myself from any of it. Life was a unitary movement, and everything was included.

Everything is sacred

In the following weeks, months and years, this realization started to turn my whole life around (and eventually led to me becoming an author and teacher). Because now I knew, and I could never truly forget: whatever is arising right now, whether it's chairs and carpets, or it's trees and cars, or it's a dog barking or a car beeping its horn, or it's waves of sadness or fear moving through the body, or the most intense and raw heartbreak upon losing a loved one, or the shattering of a dream of how things were going to turn out—on the deepest level it is all sacred, in a way the human mind will never comprehend. Nothing that happens is against life, everything is life, just as no wave can be separate from the ocean—every wave is the ocean.

Seen in the Light of oneness, even my imperfections and pains—my fears, my doubts, the things I disliked about myself, my yearnings—were so perfect! There was a sense that everything was in its right place in a way that I could never fully comprehend and didn't need to. All of my old concepts about perfection, about enlightenment, about spirituality itself, were destroyed. I'd always seen enlightenment as some kind of perfect future state, where all imperfection would be gone, and there would just be bliss all the time. This realization turned the whole thing on its head, because now perfection was all about this total embrace of imperfection, the total embrace of this moment, the deep allowing of whatever was moving here, whether it was sadness, or fear, or pain, or a longing to understand. Even a longing to understand is sacred, seen through eyes of Light.

I realized why I had suffered so deeply my whole life. My suffering had been my attempt to push experiences away, to resist the present moment, to numb myself to pain rather than allow it to move in me, to keep life at bay. I realized that my whole life I'd been on the run. I realized that the solution to depression, fear, and anxiety always lies in remembering to turn towards life, to actually begin to embrace the present moment, no matter how painful or full of uncertainty the moment is.

You see, humans have always thought in terms of abstract and conceptual mind-created opposites. God and the devil, life and death, good and evil, positive and negative, light and dark; my Truth versus your Truth, my God versus your God, my religion versus your religion, even my awakening versus your awakening! But when we were children, we saw things differently. We knew—without words—that life was a profound mystery, fascinating and full of wonder. We saw life without the labels. A flower wasn't just a flower—it was a miracle. A chair wasn't just a chair—it was alive. Everything here was mysterious in essence, and life was a great game, a play. As we grew up, we were taught, and accepted, the names for everything. We learned to say 'flower' and we learned about all the different kinds of flowers, all the facts. And we thought we 'knew' flowers, chairs, animals, people, because we knew their names. We forgot that the names were just thoughts, arbitrary bits of information, sounds we had been taught, and thoughts could never capture reality, and underneath our conceptual overlay of thinking, reality is always a mystery. Reality is too vast, too mysterious, too alive, too immediate to be captured by thought. Just look up at the stars at night, and you will understand.

Not only did we name everything around us, but we also named our own intimate 'inner' experiences. We started to label our own private feelings, the mystery of life that moved in us. 'Sadness,' we learned to call it. 'Anger.' 'Fear.' 'Frustration.' 'Joy.' 'Boredom.' 'Longing.' And then perhaps we were told that anger was 'bad,' and sadness was 'negative,' and certain desires were 'impure,' and so on. So not only had we slapped labels on our most intimate experiences, but now we had added another layer: judgment, opinion, rejection. Certain parts of ourselves we called negative, and certain parts we called positive. And then an inner war began. The good me versus the bad me. The healthy me versus the unhealthy me. The saint versus the sinner. The ignorant one versus the enlightened one. The positive one against the negative one. We tried to get rid of the negative in us, tried to be 'good' and 'pure' and 'holy' and even 'enlightened,' and we split ourselves in two, and then dreamt of union.

Without the words, without the labels, without the thought-created stories, do we really have any way of knowing what we are experiencing right now? Take away the label 'fear,' and what is it that moves in you right now? Is it really 'dark' against light? Take away the description 'sadness,' and what is it? Is it really 'negative?' Remove the concept 'anger' and what is this raw life energy that pulsates in you? Become curious. Allow your present experience to become totally fascinating. Stop calling the energy 'positive' or 'negative,' 'light' or 'dark,' 'right' or 'wrong,' 'healthy' or 'unhealthy,' and what is there? Come back to the sensations in the body. Tingly, alive sensations—prickly, dull, warm, intense, fluttery—dancing in the belly, chest, throat, head. Feel life in the raw, without judgment. Let all energies move in you, without labeling them or pushing them away. This is the secret of healing.

The present moment

We spend so much of our lives running away from the present moment, furiously working on ourselves, trying to become better, faster, more successful, more loveable, even more enlightened. But at some point we start to question, where is this all leading? Is happiness really somewhere in the future? Is life all about getting 'there?' What about here, the place we stand? What about this moment, where we have our being? When we come out of the story of our lives, our heavy pasts and imagined futures, and bring our attention back to the present moment, the Now (which is all we can really know), we may find ourselves becoming fascinated, curious, with the sensations of the body, with the sounds in the room we're in, with what is alive where we are. We may begin to realize that true happiness is about coming alive to this moment, and embracing ourselves, warts and all, with all our imperfections, doubts—seeing ourselves as perfect expressions of life.

The realization that happiness does not lie outside ourselves has huge implications for our relationships. We no longer look towards other people—parents, lovers, authority figures—to make us happy. We no longer seek our completion through other people. At the same time, we can no longer blame anyone else for our unhappiness. So much conflict in our relationships comes down to seeking from other people what they can never give us, from blaming others for our dissatisfaction and longings. As the spiritual teacher Eckhart Tolle says, "Relationships do not cause pain and unhappiness. They bring out the pain and unhappiness that is already in you."

As we stop seeking outside of ourselves for happiness, we learn to honor what is alive in us, to embrace our thoughts and feelings the way we would embrace a newborn baby. Every thought, every feeling, however intense, is a movement of life—not a threat to you, but something in you that wants to be acknowledged, touched, loved, allowed. Nobody else is responsible for your feelings! Yes, others may trigger unresolved pain and sorrow in you, they may contribute to the field in which your old, unprocessed pain can resurface, but they cannot make you feel how you feel. Nobody can make you happy, nobody can make you unhappy, and this can be a hard Truth to swallow at first, because it means there is nobody to

Other Books in The Light Series
☼

The Light: A Book of Wisdom
How to Lead An Enlightened Life Filled With
Love, Joy, Truth, and Beauty

Experiences from the Light
Ordinary People's Extraordinary Experiences
of Transformation, Miracles, and Spiritual
Awakening

Coming soon in the Light series
☼

The Light: A Book of Truth
[part three of *The Light* series]

Help us Spread the Light!

Here are three quick ways in which you can help us spread the Light, once you have finished reading this book:

1. Write a review about *The Light: A Book of Knowing* on Amazon.com or the website of another online seller.

2. Tell five friends about *The Light: A Book of Knowing*.

3. Tell your local bookshop about *The Light: A Book of Knowing* and suggest that they order some copies.

Free Bonuses!

Get your FREE LIGHT BONUSES by going to
www.thelightnetwork.com/bonuses